THE FRENCH REVOLUTION

THE FRENCH REVOLUTION

BY

HILAIRE BELLOC

CAVALIER BOOKS
MILWAUKEE, WISCONSIN

Copyright 1911 by Hilaire Belloc.
First published by Henry Holt and Company, New York, 1911.
Republished by Cavalier Books, Milwaukee, 2018.
Cover: *Louis XVI, King of France and Navarre*
by Antoine-François Callet, 1789.

ISBN: 978-1-948231-02-2

Cavalier Books

PREFACE

The object of these few pages is not to recount once more the history of the Revolution: that can be followed in any one of a hundred text-books. Their object is rather to lay, if that be possible, an explanation of it before the English reader; so that he may understand both what it was and how it proceeded, and also why certain problems hitherto unfamiliar to Englishmen have risen out of it.

First, therefore, it is necessary to set down, clearly without modern accretion, that political theory which was a sort of religious creed, supplying the motive force of the whole business; of the new Civil Code as of the massacres; of the panics and capitulations as of the victories; of the successful transformation of society as of the conspicuous failures in detail which still menace the achievement of the Revolution.

This grasped, the way in which the main events followed each other, and the reason of their interlocking and proceeding as they did must be put forward—not, I repeat, in the shape of a chronicle, but in the shape of a thesis. Thus the reader must know not only that the failure of the royal family's flight was followed by war, but how and why it was followed by war. He must not only appreciate the severity of the government of the great Committee, but why that severity was present, and of the conditions of war upon which it reposed. But in so explaining the development of the movement it is necessary to select for appreciation as the chief figures the characters of the time, since upon their will and manner depended the fate of the whole. For instance, had the Queen been French either in blood or in sympathy, had the King been alert, had any one character retained the old religious motives, all history would have been changed, and this human company must be seen if its action and drama are to be comprehended.

The reader interested in that capital event should further seize (and but too rarely has an opportunity for seizing) its military aspect; and this difficulty of his proceeds from two causes: the first, that historians, even when they recognise the importance of the military side of some past movement, are careless of the military aspect, and think it sufficient to relate particular victories and general actions. The military aspect of any period does not consist in these, but in the campaigns of which actions, however decisive, are but incidental parts. In other words, the reader must seize the movement and design of armies if he is to seize a military period, and these are not commonly given him. In the second place, the historian, however much alive to the importance of military affairs, too rarely presents them as part of a general position. He will make his story a story of war, or again, a story of civilian development, and the reader will fail to see how the two combine.

Now, the Revolution, more than any other modern period, turns upon, and is explained by, its military history. On this account has so considerable a space been devoted to the explaining of that feature.

The reader will note, again, that the quarrel between the Revolution and the Catholic Church has also been dealt with at length.

To emphasise this aspect of the revolutionary struggle may seem unusual and perhaps deserves a word of apology.

The reader is invited to consider the fact that the Revolution took place in a country which had, in the first place, definitely determined during the religious struggle of the sixteenth and seventeenth centuries to remain in communion with Rome; and had, in the second place, admitted a very large and important body of converts to the doctrines of the Reformation.

The determination of the French people, in the crisis of 1572–1610, to remain Catholic under a strong central Government, was a capital point in the future history of France. So was the presence of a wealthy, very large, and highly cultivated body of dissentients in the midst of the nation. The two phenomena hardly co-existed elsewhere in Europe. Between them they lent to the political history of France a peculiar character which the nineteenth century, even more than the Revolution itself, has emphasised; and it is the opinion of the present writer that it is impossible to understand the Revolution unless very high relief is given to the religious problem.

If a personal point may be noted, the fact that the writer of these pages is himself a Catholic and in political sympathy strongly attached to the political theory of the Revolution, should not be hidden from the reader. Such personal conditions have perhaps enabled him to treat the matter more thoroughly than it might have been treated by one who rejected either Republicanism upon the one hand, or Catholicism upon the other; but he believes that no personal and therefore exaggerated note has been allowed to intrude upon his description of what is a definite piece of objective history lying in the field of record rather than in that of opinion.

Some years ago the paramount importance of the quarrel between the Church and the Revolution might still have been questioned by men who had no personal experience of the struggle, and of its vast results. To-day the increasing consequences and the contemporary violence of that quarrel make its presentation an essential part of any study of the period.

The scheme thus outlined will show why I have given this sketch the divisions in which it lies.

H. BELLOC.

King's Land,
January, 1911.

CONTENTS

CHAPTER I

THE POLITICAL THEORY OF THE REVOLUTION

The political theory upon which the Revolution proceeded has, especially in this country, suffered ridicule as local, as ephemeral, and as fallacious. It is universal, it is eternal, and it is true.

It may be briefly stated thus: that a political community pretending to sovereignty, that is, pretending to a moral right of defending its existence against all other communities, derives the civil and temporal authority of its laws not from its actual rulers, nor even from its magistracy, but from itself.

But the community cannot express authority unless it possesses *corporate initiative*; that is, unless the mass of its component units are able to combine for the purpose of a common expression, are conscious of a common will, and have something in common which makes the whole sovereign indeed.

It may be that this power of corporate initiative and of corresponding corporate expression is forbidden to men. In that case no such thing as a sovereign community can be said to exist. In that case "patriotism," "public opinion," "the genius of a people," are terms without meaning. But the human race in all times and in all places has agreed that such terms have meaning, and the conception that a community can so live, order and be itself, is a human conception as consonant to the nature of man as is his sense of right and wrong; it is much more intimately a part of that nature than are the common accidents determining human life, such as nourishment, generation or repose: nay, more intimate a part of it than anything which attaches to the body.

This theory of political morals, though subject to a limitless degradation in practice, underlies the argument of every man who pretends to regard the conduct of the State as a business affecting the

11

conscience of citizens. Upon it relies every protest against tyranny and every denunciation of foreign aggression.

He that is most enamoured of some set machinery for the government of men, and who regards the sacramental function of an hereditary monarch (as in Russia), the organic character of a native oligarchy (as in England), the mechanical arrangement of election by majorities, or even in a crisis the intense conviction and therefore the intense activity and conclusive power of great crowds as salutary to the State, will invariably, if any one of these engines fail him in the achievement of what he desires for his country, fall back upon the doctrine of an ultimately sovereign community. He will complain that though an election has defeated his ideal, yet true national tradition and true national sentiment were upon his side. If he defends the action of a native oligarchy against the leaders of the populace, he does so by an explanation (more or less explicit) that the oligarchy is more truly national, that is more truly communal, than the engineered expression of opinion of which the demagogues (as he will call them) have been the mouthpieces. Even in blaming men for criticising or restraining an hereditary monarch the adherent of that monarch will blame them upon the ground that their action is anti-national, that is anti-communal; and, in a word, no man pretending to sanity can challenge in matters temporal and civil the ultimate authority of whatever is felt to be (though with what difficulty is it not defined!) the general civic sense which builds up a State.

Those words "civil" and "temporal" must lead the reader to the next consideration; which is, that the last authority of all does not reside even in the community.

It must be admitted by all those who have considered their own nature and that of their fellow beings that the ultimate authority in any act is God. Or if the name of God sound unusual in an English publication to-day, then what now takes the place of it for many (an imperfect phrase), "the moral sense."

Thus if there be cast together in some abandoned place a community of a few families so depraved or so necessitous that, against the teachings of their own consciences, and well knowing that what they are doing is what we call *wrong*, yet they will unanimously agree to do it, then that agreement of theirs, though certainly no temporal or civil authority can be quoted against it, is yet unjustifiable. Another authority lies behind. Still more evidently would this be true if, of say,

twelve, seven decided (knowing the thing to be wrong) that the wrong
thing should be done, five stood out for the right—and yet the majority possessed by the seven should be determined a sufficient authority
for the wrongful command.

But it is to be noted that this axiom only applies where the authority of the moral law (God, as the author of this book, with due defer-
ence to his readers, would prefer to say) is recognised and yet flouted.
If those twelve families do sincerely believe such and such a general
action to be right, then not only is their authority when they carry
it into practice a civil and a temporal authority; it is an authority
absolute in all respects; and further, if, upon a division of opinion
among them not perhaps a bare majority, nay, perhaps not a majority
at all, but at any rate a determinant current of opinion—determinant
in intensity and in weight, that is, as well as in numbers—declares an
action to be right, then that determinant weight of opinion gives to its
resolve a political authority not only civil and temporal but absolute.
Beyond it and above it there is no appeal.

In other words, men may justly condemn, and justly have in a
thousand circumstances condemned, the theory that a mere decision
on the major part of the community was necessarily right in morals.
It is, for that matter, self-evident that if one community decides in one
fashion, another, also sovereign, in the opposite fashion, both cannot
be right. Reasoning men have also protested, and justly, against the
conception that what a majority in numbers, or even (what is more
compelling still) a unanimity of decision in a community may order,
may not only be wrong but may be something which that community has no authority to order since, though it possesses a civil and
temporal authority, it acts against that ultimate authority which is its
own consciousness of right. Men may and do justly protest against the
doctrine that a community is incapable of doing deliberate evil; it is
as capable of such an action as is an individual. But men nowhere do
or can deny that the community acting as it thinks right is ultimately
sovereign: there is no alternative to so plain a truth.

Let us take it, then, as indubitable that where civil government is
concerned, the community is supreme, if only from the argument that
no organ within the community can prove its right to withstand the
corporate will when once that corporate will shall find expression.

All arguments which are advanced against this prime axiom of
political ethics are, when they are analysed, found to repose upon a

confusion of thought. Thus a man will say, "This doctrine would lead my country to abandon her suzerainty over that other nation, but were I to consent to this, I should be weakening my country, to which I owe allegiance." The doctrine compels him to no such muddlement. The community of which he is a member is free to make its dispositions for safety, and is bound to preserve its own life. It is for the oppressed to protest and to rebel.

Similarly, men think that this doctrine in some way jars with the actual lethargy and actual imbecility of men in their corporate action. It does nothing of the kind. This lethargy, that imbecility, and all the other things that limit the application of the doctrine, in no way touch its right reason, any more than the fact that the speech of all men is imperfect contradicts the principle that man has a moral right to self-expression. That a dumb man cannot speak at all, but must write, is, so far from a contradiction, a proof of the truth that speech is the prime expression of man; and in the same way a community utterly without the power of expressing its corporate will is no contradiction, but a proof, of the general rule that such expression and the imposing of such decisions are normal to mankind. The very oddity of the contrast between the abnormal and the normal aids us in our decision, and when we see a people conquered and not persuaded, yet making no attempt at rebellion, or a people free from foreign oppression yet bewildered at the prospect of self-government, the oddity of the phenomenon proves our rule.

But though all this be true, there stands against the statement of our political axiom not a contradiction added, but a criticism; and all men with some knowledge of their fellows and of themselves at once perceive, *first*, that the psychology of corporate action differs essentially from the psychology of individual action, and *secondly*, that in proportion to the number, the discussions, the lack of intimacy, and in general the friction of the many, corporate action by a community, corporate self-realisation and the imposition of a corporate will, varies from the difficult to the impossible.

On this no words need be wasted. All men who reason and who observe are agreed that, in proportion to distance, numbers, and complexity, the difficulty of self-expression within a community increases. We may get in a lively people explosions of popular will violent, acute, and certainly real; but rare. We may attempt with a people more lethargic to obtain some reflection of popular will through the medium of a permanent machinery of deputation which, less than any other, perhaps, permits a great community to express itself truly. We may rely upon the national sympathies of an aristocracy or of a king. But in any case we know that large communities can only indirectly and imperfectly express themselves where the permanent government of their whole interest is concerned. Our attachment, which may be passionate, to the rights of the Common Will we must satisfy either by demanding a loose federation of small, self-governing states, or submitting the central government of large ones to occasional insurrection and to violent corporate expressions of opinion which shall readjust the relations between the governor and the governed.

All this is true: but such a criticism of the theory in political morals which lay behind the Revolution, the theory that the community is sovereign, is no contradiction. It only tells us that pure right cannot act untrammelled in human affairs and that it acts in some conditions more laboriously than in others: it gives not a jot of authority to any alternative thesis.*

Such is the general theory of the Revolution to which the command of Jean Jacques Rousseau over the French tongue gave imperishable expression in that book whose style and logical connection may be compared to some exact and strong piece of engineering. He entitled it the *Contrat Social*, and it became the formula of the Revolutionary Creed. But though no man, perhaps, has put the prime truth of political morals so well, that truth was as old as the world; it appears in the passionate rhetoric of a hundred leaders and has stood at the head or has been woven into the laws of free States without number.

---

* We need not waste any time upon those who talk about such and such a form of government being good because "it works." The use of such language connotes that the user of it is fatigued by the effort of thought. For what is "working," *i.e.* successful action, in any sphere? The attainment of certain ends in that sphere. What are those ends in a State? If material well-being, then there is an end to talk of patriotism, the nation, public opinion and the rest of it which, as we all very well know, men always have regarded and always will regard as the supreme matters of public interest. If the end is not material well-being, but a sense of political freedom and of the power of the citizen to react upon the State, then to say that an institution "works" though apparently not democratic, is simply to say that under such and such conditions that institution achieves the ends of democracy most nearly. In other words, to contrast the good "working" of an institution superficially undemocratic with democratic theory is meaningless. The institution "works" in proportion as it satisfies that political sense which perfect democracy would, were it attainable, completely satisfy.

In the English language the Declaration of Independence is perhaps its noblest expression. And though this document was posterior to the great work of Rousseau and (through the genius of Jefferson) was in some part descended from it, its language, and still more the actions of those who drafted and supported it, are sufficient to explain what I mean to English readers.

Now with this general theory there stand connected on the one hand certain great principles without which it would have no meaning, and also on the other hand a number of minor points concerning no more than the machinery of politics. The first are vital to democracy. The second, in spite of their great popularity at the time of the Revolution and of the sanction which the Revolution gave them, nay, of their universality since the Revolution, have in reality nothing to do with the revolutionary theory itself.

Of these two categories the type of the first is the doctrine of the equality of man; the type of the second is the mere machinery called "representative."

The doctrine of the equality of the man is a transcendent doctrine: a "dogma," as we call such doctrines in the field of transcendental religion. It corresponds to no physical reality which we can grasp, it is hardly to be adumbrated even by metaphors drawn from physical objects. We may attempt to rationalise it by saying that what is common to all men is not *more* important but *infinitely more* important than the accidents by which men differ. We may compare human attributes to tri-dimensional, and personal attributes to bi-dimensional measurements; we may say that whatever man has of his nature is the standard of man, and we may show that in all such things men are potentially equal. None of these metaphors explains the matter; still less do any of them satisfy the demand of those to whom the dogma may be incomprehensible.

Its truth is to be arrived at (for these) in a negative manner. If men are *not* equal then no scheme of jurisprudence, no act of justice, no movement of human indignation, no exaltation of fellowship, has any meaning. The doctrine of the equality of man is one which, like many of the great transcendental doctrines, may be proved by the results consequent upon its absence. It is in man to believe it—and all lively societies believe it.

It is certainly not in man to prove the equality of men save, as I have said, by negation; but it demands no considerable intellectual faculty to perceive that, void of the doctrine of equality, the conception of political freedom and of a community's moral right to self-government disappear. Now to believe that doctrine positively, and to believe it ardently, to go on crusade for that religious point, was indeed characteristic of the French. It required the peculiar and inherited religious temper of the French which had for so many hundred years seized and defined point after point in the character of man, to grow enamoured of this definition and to feel it not in the intellect, but as it were in their bones. They became soldiers for it, and that enormous march of theirs, overrunning Europe, which may not inaptly be compared to their adventures in the twelfth century, when they engaged upon the Crusades, was inspired by no one part of the doctrine of political freedom more strongly than by this doctrine of equality.

The scorn which was in those days universally felt for that pride which associates itself with things not inherent to a man (notably and most absurdly with capricious differences of wealth) never ran higher; and the passionate sense of justice which springs from this profound and fundamental social dogma of equality, as it moved France during the Revolution to frenzy, so also moved it to creation. Those who ask how it was that a group of men sustaining all the weight of civil conflict within and of universal war without, yet made time enough in twenty years to frame the codes which govern modern Europe, to lay down the foundations of universal education, of a strictly impersonal scheme of administration, and even in detail to remodel the material face of society—in a word, to make modern Europe—must be content for their reply to learn that the Republican Energy had for its flame and excitant this vision: a sense almost physical of the equality of man.

The minor points which wove themselves into the political practice of democracy during the Revolution, which are not of its principles, and which would not, were they abstracted, affect its essence, are of quite another and less noble kind. I have taken as the chief of these the machinery of deputation or of "representation."

The representative system had been designed for a particular purpose under the influence of the Church and especially of the monastic orders (who invented it) in the Middle Ages. It had been practised as a useful check upon the national monarchy in France, and as a useful form of national expression in times of crisis or when national initiative was peculiarly demanded.

In Spain it became, as the Middle Ages proceeded, a very vital national and local thing, varying from place to place. It is not surprising that Spain (seeing that in her territory the first experiments in representation were made) should have thus preserved it, popular and alive.

In England Representation, vigorous as everywhere else in the true Middle Ages, narrowed and decayed at their close, until in the seventeenth century it had become a mere scheme for aristocratic government.

In France for nearly two hundred years before the Revolution it had fallen into disuse, but an active memory of it still remained; especially a memory of its value in critical moments when a consultation of the whole people was required, and when the corporate initiative of the whole people must be set at work in order to save the State.

It is no wonder, therefore, that the French, on the eve of the Revolution, clamoured for a revival of representation, or, as the system was called in the French tongue, "the States-General." But as a permanent machine of government no one in Europe had the least idea how the system might serve the ends of democracy. In England democracy was not practised nor was representation connected with the conception of it. The nation had forgotten democracy as completely as it had forgotten the religion and the old ideals of the Middle Ages.

In those parts of Christendom in which this ancient Christian institution of a parliament had not narrowed to be the mask of an oligarchy or dwindled to be a mere provincial custom, its use had disappeared. The ancient function of Representation, when it had been most lively and vigorous, that is, in the Middle Ages, was occasionally to initiate a national policy in critical moments, but more generally to grant taxes. What a democratic parliament might do, no one in 1789 could conceive.

There was indeed one great example of democratic representation in existence: the example of the United States; but the conditions were wholly different from those of Europe. No true central power yet existed there; no ancient central institution, no Crown nor any Custom of the City. The numbers over which American representative democracy then held power were not to be compared to the twenty-five millions who inhabited the French realm. And even so, most of what counted in their lives was regulated by a system of highly local autonomy: for they were as scattered as they were few, and the wisest and strongest and best were dependent upon slaves. In Europe, I repeat, the experiment was untried; and it is one of the chief faults of the French revolutionaries that, having been compelled in the critical moment of the opening of the Revolution to the use of election and representation, they envisaged the permanent use of a similar machinery as a something sacred to and normal in the democratic State.

True, they could not foresee modern parliamentarism. Nothing could be more alien to their conception of the State than the deplorable method of government which parliamentarism everywhere tends to introduce to-day.

True, the French people during the revolutionary wars made short work of parliamentary theory, and found it a more national thing to follow a soldier (being by that time all soldiers themselves), and to incarnate in a dictator the will of the nation.

But though the French revolutionaries could not have foreseen what we call "Parliamentarism" to-day, and though the society from which they sprang made short work of the oligarchic pretensions of a parliament when the realities of the national struggle had to be considered, yet they did as a fact pay an almost absurd reverence to the machinery of representation and election.

They went so far as to introduce it into their attempted reform of the Church; they introduced it everywhere into civil government, from the smallest units to the highest. They even for a moment played with the illusion in that most real of games which men can ever play at—the business of arms: they allowed the election of officers. They were led to do this by that common fallacy, more excusable in them than in us, which confounds the individual will with the corporate. A representative (they thought) could in some way be the permanent receptacle of his electorate. They imagined that corporate initiative was always sufficiently active, in no matter what divisions or subdivisions, to react at once upon the delegate, to guide him as may be guided a driven animal, or to command him as may be commanded a servant.

It was in vain that Rousseau, the great exponent of the democratic theory upon which France attempted to proceed, had warned posterity against the possible results of the representative system: they fell into the error, and it possesses many of their descendants to this day.

Rousseau's searching mind perceived indeed no more than the general truth that men who consent to a representative system are free only while the representatives are not sitting. But (as is so often the case with intuitions of genius) though he saw not the whole of the evil, he had put his finger upon its central spot, and from that main and just principle which he laid down—that under a merely representative system men cannot be really free—flow all those evils which we now know to attach to this method of government. What a rather clumsy epigram has called "the audacity of elected persons" is part of this truth. The evident spectacle of modern parliamentary nations driven against their will into economic conditions which appal them, proceeds again from the same truth; the conspicuous and hearty contempt into which parliamentary institutions have everywhere fallen again proceeds from it, and there proceeds from it that further derivative plague that the representatives themselves have now everywhere become more servile than the electorate and that in all parliamentary countries a few intriguers are the unworthy depositories of power, and by their service of finance permit the money-dealers to govern us all to-day. Rousseau, I say, the chief prophet of the Revolution, had warned the French of this danger. It is a capital example of his talent, for the experiment of democratic representation had not yet, in his time, been tried. But much more is that power of his by which he not only stamped and issued the gold of democracy as it had never till then been minted. No one man makes a people or their creed, but Rousseau more than any other man made vocal the creed of a people, and it is advisable or necessary for the reader of the Revolution to consider at the outset of his reading of what nature was Rousseau's abundant influence upon the men who remodelled the society of Europe between 1789 and 1794.

Why did he dominate those five years, and how was it that he dominated them increasingly?

An explanation of Rousseau's power merits a particular digression, for few who express themselves in the English tongue have cared to understand it, and in the academies provincial men have been content to deal with this great writer as though he were in some way inferior to themselves.

CHAPTER II

ROUSSEAU

In order to appreciate what Rousseau meant to the revolutionary movement, it is necessary to consider the effect of style upon men.

Men are influenced by the word. Spoken or written, the *word* is the organ of persuasion and, therefore, of moral government.

Now, degraded as that term has become in our time, there is no proper term to express the exact use of words save the term "style."

What words we use, and in what order we put them, is the whole matter of style; and a man desiring to influence his fellow men has therefore not one, but two co-related instruments at his disposal. He cannot use one without the other. The weakness of the one will ruin the other. These two instruments are his idea and his style.

However powerful, native, sympathetic to his hearers' mood or cogently provable by reference to new things may be a man's idea, he cannot persuade his fellow men to it if he have not words that express it. And he will persuade them more and more in proportion as his words are well chosen and in the right order, such order being determined by the genius of the language whence they are drawn.

Whether the idea of which Rousseau made himself the exponent in his famous tract be true or false, need not further concern us in this little book. We all know that the difficult attempt to realise political freedom has attracted various communities of men at various times and repelled others. What English readers rarely hear is that the triumph of Rousseau depended not only on the first element in persuasion, which is vision, but also upon the second of the two co-related instruments by which a man may influence his fellows—to wit, style. It was his choice of French words and the order in which he arranged them, that gave him his enormous ascendancy over the generation which was young when he was old.

I have alluded to his famous tract, the *Contrat Social*, and here a second point concerning it may be introduced. This book which gave a text for the Revolution, the document to which its political theory could refer, was by no means (as foreign observers have sometimes imagined) the whole body of writing for which Rousseau was responsible. To imagine that is to make the very common error of confusing a man with his books.

Rousseau wrote on many things: his character was of an exalted, nervous and diseased sort. Its excessive sensibility degenerated with advancing years into something not distinguishable from mania. He wrote upon education, and the glory of his style carried conviction both where he was right and where the short experience of a hundred years has proved him to have been wholly wrong. He wrote upon love, and half the lessons to be drawn from his writing will be condemned by the sane. He wrote upon botany at vast length; he wrote also upon music—with what success in either department I am incompetent to determine. He wrote upon human inequality: and though the sentences were beautiful and the sentiment just, the analysis was very insufficient and the historical conception bad. He wrote upon a project for perpetual peace, which was rubbish; and he wrote upon the government of Poland an essay which was a perfect masterpiece.

But when a great writer writes, each of his great writings has a life of its own, and it was not any of these other writings of Rousseau, on love or botany, which were the text of the Revolution. The text of the Revolution was his *Contrat Social*.

Now it is not too much to say that never in the history of political theory has a political theory been put forward so lucidly, so convincingly, so tersely or so accurately as in this short and wonderful book. The modern publisher in this country would be ashamed to print it: not for its views (which would now seem commonplace), nor for its excellence, which would ensure it a failure, but for its brevity. It is as short as a gospel, and would cover but a hundred pages of one of our serious reviews. A modern publisher in this city would not know what price to set upon such a work, and the modern reader in this country would be puzzled to understand how a great thing could be got within so narrow a compass. A debate in Parliament or the libretto of a long pantomime is of greater volume.

Nevertheless, if it be closely read the *Contrat Social* will be discovered to say all that can be said of the moral basis of democracy. Our ignorance of the historical basis of the State is presumed in the very opening lines of it. The logical priority of the family to the State is the next statement. The ridiculous and shameful argument that strength is the basis of authority—which has never had standing save among the uninstructed or the superficial—is contemptuously dismissed in a very simple proof which forms the third chapter, and that chapter is not a page of a book in length. It is with the fifth chapter that the powerful argument begins, and the logical precedence of *human association* to any particular form of government is the foundation stone of that analysis. It is this indeed which gives its title to the book: the moral authority of men in community arises from *conscious association*; or, as an exact phraseology would have it, a "social contract." All the business of democracy as based upon the only moral authority in a State follows from this first principle, and is developed in Rousseau's extraordinary achievement which, much more than any other writing not religious, has affected the destiny of mankind.

It is indeed astonishing to one who is well acquainted not only with the matter, but with the manner of the *Contrat Social*, to remark what criticisms have been passed upon it by those who either have not read the work or, having read it, did so with an imperfect knowledge of the meaning of French words. The two great counter arguments, the one theoretic the other practical, which democracy has to meet, stand luminously exposed in these pages, though in so short a treatise the author might have been excused from considering them. The theoretical argument against democracy is, of course, that man being prone to evil, something external to him and indifferent to his passions must be put up to govern him; the people will corrupt themselves, but a despot or an oligarchy, when it has satisfied its corrupt desires, still has a wide margin over which it may rule well because it is indifferent. You cannot bribe the despot or the oligarch beyond the limit of his desires, but a whole people can follow its own corrupt desires to the full, and they will infect all government.

The full practice of democracy, therefore, says Rousseau, is better suited to angels than to men.

As to the practical argument that men are not sufficiently conscious of the State to practise democracy, save in small communities, that plea also is recognised and stated better than any one else has stated it. For there is not in this book an apology for democracy as a method of government, but a statement of why and how democracy is right.

The silly confusion which regards a representative method as essentially democratic has never been more contemptuously dealt with, nor more thoroughly, than in the few words in which the *Contrat Social* dismisses it for ever; though it was left to our own time to discover, in the school of unpleasant experience, how right was Rousseau in this particular condemnation.

Exiguous as are the limits within which the great writer has finally decided the theory of democracy, he finds space for side issues which nowhere else but in this book had been orderly considered, and which, when once one has heard them mentioned, one sees to be of the most excellent wisdom: that the fundamental laws, or original and particular bonds, of a new democracy must come from a source external to itself; that to the nature of the people for whom one is legislating, however democratic the form of the State, we must conform the particulars of law; that a democracy cannot live without "tribunes"; that no utterly inflexible law can be permitted in the State—and hence the necessity for dictatorship in exceptional times; that no code can foresee future details—and so forth.

It would be a legitimate and entertaining task to challenge any man who had not read the *Contrat Social* (and this would include most academic writers upon the treatise) to challenge any such one, I say, to put down an argument against democratic theory which could not be found within those few pages, or to suggest a limitation of it which Rousseau had not touched on.

If proof were needed of what particular merits this pamphlet displayed, it would be sufficient to point out that in a time when the problem represented by religion was least comprehended, when the practice of religion was at its lowest, and when the meaning, almost, of religion had left men's minds, Rousseau was capable of writing his final chapter.

That the great religious revival of the nineteenth century should have proved Rousseau's view of religion in the State to be insufficient is in no way remarkable, for when Rousseau wrote, that revival was undreamt of; what is remarkable is that he should have allowed as he did for the religious sentiment, and above all, that he should have seen how impossible it is for a selection of Christian dogma to be accepted as a civic religion.

It is further amazing that at such a time a man could be found who should appreciate that for the State, to have unity, it must possess a religion, and Rousseau's attempt to define that minimum or substratum of religion without which unity could not exist in the State unfortunately became the commonplace of the politicians, and particularly of the English politicians who succeeded him. Who might not think, for instance, that he was reading—though better expressed, of course, than a politician could put it—some "Liberal" politician at Westminster, if he were to come on such phrases as these with regard to what should be taught in the schools of the country?

"The doctrines taught by the State should be simple, few in number, expressed with precision and without explanation or commentary. The existence of a powerful God, beneficent, providential and good; the future life; the happiness of the good and the punishment of evil; the sanctity of the agreements which bind society together and of laws; while as for negative doctrines, one is sufficient, and that one is the wickedness of intolerance."

Rousseau's hundred pages are the direct source of the theory of the modern State; their lucidity and unmatched economy of diction; their rigid analysis, their epigrammatic judgment and wisdom—these are the reservoirs from whence modern democracy has flowed; what are now proved to be the errors of democracy are errors against which the *Contrat Social* warned men; the moral apology of democracy is the moral apology written by Rousseau; and if in this one point of religion he struck a more confused and a less determined note than in the rest, it must be remembered that in his time no other man understood what part religion played in human affairs; for in his days the few who studied religion and observed it could not connect it in any way with the political nature of man, and of those who counted in the intellect of Europe, by far the greater number thought political problems better solved if religion (which they had lost) were treated as negligible. They were wrong—and Rousseau, in his generalities upon the soul, was insufficient; both were beneath the height of a final theory of man, but Rousseau came much nearer to comprehension, even in this point of religion, than did any of his contemporaries.

CHAPTER III

THE CHARACTERS OF THE REVOLUTION

KING LOUIS XVI

As might be expected, the character of King Louis XVI has suffered more distortion at the hands of historians than has any other of the revolutionary figures; and this because he combined with that personal character of his a certain office to which were traditionally attached certain points of view and methods of action which the historian takes for granted when he deals with the character of the man. As any one thinking of a judge of some standing upon the English bench cannot but believe that he is possessed of some learning or some gravity, etc.; as any one hearing of a famous soldier cannot but believe that he has certain qualities associated with the business of soldiering, so historians tend to confuse the personality and character of Louis XVI with that of his office; they either by contrast exaggerate his unkingly defects or by sympathy exaggerate his kingly opposition to reform.

The student will do well to avoid this error and its source, and to think of Louis as of a man who had been casually introduced, almost without preparation, into the office which he held. In other words, the student will do well, in his reading of the Revolution, to consider Louis XVI simply as a man, and his character as a private character. For this last of the long, unbroken line of Capetians possessed a character essentially individual. It was of a type which, no matter what accidents of fortune might have fallen upon its possessor, would have remained the same. Nor was ever a man possessed of high office whom high office had less moulded.

Men thus impervious to their environment are commonly so from two causes: either from an intense and vivid personal initiative which may border upon madness, or from something thick and heavy in their moral accoutrement which defends against external action the inner personal temperament. The latter was the case with Louis.

He was very slow of thought, and very slow of decision. His physical movements were slow. The movement of his eyes was notably slow. He had a way of falling asleep under the effort of fatigue at the most incongruous moments. The things that amused him were of the largest and most superficial kind. Horse-play, now and then a little touched with eccentricity, and very plain but unexpected jokes. One may express him from one aspect by saying that he was one of those men whom you could never by any chance have hoped to convince of anything. The few things which he accepted he accepted quite simply, and the process of reasoning in the mouth of any who approached him was always too rapid for him to follow. But it must not be imagined on this account that the moral integument so described was wrapped about a void. On the contrary, it enclosed a very definite character. Louis possessed a number of intimate convictions upon which he was not to be shaken. He was profoundly convinced of the existence and value of a certain corporate tradition in the organism which he ruled: the French nation. He was national. In this he differed from many a pedant, many a courtier, many an ecclesiastic, and many a woman about him, especially his wife.

He was, again, possessed of all the elements of the Catholic faith.

It was, indeed, a singular thing for a man of his position at such a time to hold intimately to religion, but Louis held to it. He confessed, he communicated, he attended mass, he performed his ordinary devotions—not by way of tradition or political duty, or State function, to which religious performance was now reduced in the vast majority of his wealthy contemporaries, but as an individual for whom these things had a personal value. Had he, with precisely the same interior spirit, woken in his bed some morning to find himself a country squire, and to discover that all his past kingship had been a dream of the night, he would have continued the practice of his religion as before.

Now this is a sufficiently remarkable point, for the country squire, the noble, the lawyer, the university professor of the generation immediately preceding the Revolution had, as a rule, no conception of the Catholic Church. With them the faith was dead, save in the case of a very few who made it, if one may say so without disrespect, a mania, and in their exaggerations were themselves the proofs of the depth of decay into which the Church of Gaul had fallen.

Louis XVI was possessed, then, of religion: it appeared in many of his acts, in his hesitation to appoint not a few of the many atheist bishops of the time, in his real agony of responsibility upon the Civil Constitution of the clergy, and in nothing more than the peculiar sobriety and solid ritual whereby he prepared for a tragic, sudden, and ignominious death.

It is next to be observed that though he was a man not yet in middle age, and though he was quite devoid of ardour in any form, he had from the first matured a great basis of courage. It is well to admit that this quality in him was connected with those slow processes of thought and action which hampered him, but it is not to be explained by them. No man yet has become brave through mere stupidity.

It was not only the accidents of the Revolution that proved this quality in him: his physical habits proved it long before. He was a resolute and capable rider of the horse: an aptitude in that exercise is impossible to the coward. Again, in those by-products of courage which are apparent, even where no physical danger threatens, he was conspicuous; he had no hesitation in facing a number of men, and he had aptitude in a mechanical trade—a business by no means unconnected with virility.

Now in mentioning his virility, it is of prime importance for the student to remember, though the matter can be touched upon but lightly, that Louis, in this department of physical life, suffered from a mechanical impediment which gravely distorted the first years of his marriage, which undoubtedly wounded his self-respect, and which was perhaps the only thing that caused him permanent anxiety. He was cured by medical aid in the summer of the year 1777, but he was already three years a king and seven years a husband before that relief came to him. The tragedy affected his whole life, and, I repeat, must never be forgotten when one considers either him or Marie Antoinette in their intimate character, and in their effect as actors in the great drama.

For the rest, the character of Louis betrayed certain ineptitudes (the word ineptitude is far more accurate in this connection than the word weakness), which ineptitudes were peculiarly fatal for the military office which he held and for the belligerent crisis which he had to meet.

Few men are possessed of the eye, the subtle sympathy, the very rapid power of decision, and the comprehension of human contrasts and differences which build up the apt leader of an armed force great or small. Most men are mediocre in the combination of these qualities. But Louis was quite exceptionally hopeless where they were concerned. He could never have seen the simplest position nor have appreciated the military aspects of any character or of any body of men. He could ride, but he could not ride at the head of a column. He was not merely bad at this trade, he was nul. Drafted as a private into a conscript army, he would never have been entrusted with the duties of a corporal. He would have been impossible as a sergeant; and, possessed of commissioned rank, ridicule would have compelled him to take his discharge.

This lack did not only, or chiefly, betray itself in his inability to meet personally the armed crisis of a revolution; it was not only, or chiefly, apparent in his complete breakdown during the assault upon the palace on the 10th of August: it was also, and much more, the disastrous cause of his inability to oversee, or even to choose, military advisers.

Those who propose in the early part of the Revolution to check the mob in Paris, are excellent commanders: but Louis does not know it. Those who succeed each other at the Ministry of War, or at the head of the armies during the active part of the revolution are various in the extreme: but they all seem one to him. Between a fop like Narbonne and a subtle, trained cavalry man like Dumouriez, Louis made no distinction. The military qualities of La Fayette (which were not to be despised) meant no more to him than does music, good or bad, to a deaf man. From the beginning to the end of the movement, the whole of the military problem escaped him.

Another hole in his character, which was of prime importance at such a time, was his inability to grasp in a clear vision any general social problem. Maps he could well comprehend, and he could well retain statistics; but the landscape, as it were, of the Revolution his protuberant and lethargic eyes completely missed. He was quite unable to see where lay danger and where support, in what large masses such and such forces were grouped, and the directions in which they were advancing, or upon which they must retreat. In this matter he was, as will be seen in a moment, the very opposite of Mirabeau, and it was on account of this weakness, or rather this form of nullity, that all Mirabeau's vision was wasted upon Louis.

Finally, he had no working comprehension of Europe. He did not even exaggerate the powers of the allies in the later phases of the Revolution when they were marching upon France. He did not either under-estimate or over-estimate the policy and naval force of Great Britain, the military resources of his own subjects, the probable sympathies of the Netherlands (anti-Austrian but Catholic), the decay of Spain, the division and impotence of the Italian Peninsula. Louis saw nothing of all these things.

One may conclude the picture (for the purposes of such a short study as this) by saying that only one coincidence could have led him through the labyrinth of the time with success. That coincidence would have been the presence at his side of a friend fully trusted from childhood, loved, as religious as himself, and yet possessing precisely those qualities which he himself lacked. Had Louis found to hand such a lieutenant, the qualities I have mentioned would have been a sort of keel and ballast which would have secured the monarchy, for he was not weak, he was not impulsive, he was not even foolish: he was only wretchedly alone in his incapacities. Certainly such a nature could trust and rely upon no one who was not of this intimate kind, and he possessed no such intimate, let alone an intimate who could command the qualities I have suggested.

Being what he was, his character is among the half-dozen which determined the Revolution to take the course which it did.

THE QUEEN

Marie Antoinette presents to history a character which it is of the highest interest to regard as a whole. It is the business of her biographers to consider that character as a whole; but in her connection with the Revolution there is but one aspect of it which is of importance, and that is the attitude which such a character was bound to take towards the French nation in the midst of which the Queen found herself.

It is the solution of the whole problem which the Queen's action sets before us to apprehend the gulf that separated her not only from the French temperament, but from a comprehension of all French society. Had she been a woman lacking in energy or in decision, this alien character in her would have been a small matter, and her ignorance of the French in every form of their activity, or rather her inability to comprehend them, would have been but a private failing productive only of certain local and immediate consequences, and not in any way determining the great lines of the revolutionary movement.

As it was, her energy was not only abundant but steadfast; it grew more secure in its action as it increased with her years, and the initiative which gave that energy its course never vacillated, but was always direct. She knew her own mind, and she attempted, often with a partial success, to realise her convictions. There was no character in touch with the Executive during the first years of the Revolution comparable to hers for fixity of purpose and definition of view.

It was due to this energy and singleness of aim that her misunderstanding of the material with which she had to deal was of such fatal importance.

It was she who chose, before the outbreak of the Revolution, the succession of those ministers both Liberal and Reactionary, whose unwise plans upon either side precipitated violence. It was she who called and then revoked, and later recalled to office the wealthy and over-estimated Necker; she who substituted for him, and then so inopportunely threw over Calonne, the most national of the precursors of the Revolution, and ever after her most bitter enemy; it was she who advised the more particularly irritating details of resistance after the meeting of the first revolutionary Parliament; it was she who presided over (and helped to warp) the plans for the flight of the royal family; it was she who, after this flight had failed, framed a definite scheme for the coercion of the French people by the Governments of Europe; it was she who betrayed to foreign chanceries the French plan of campaign when war had become inevitable; finally, it was she who inspired the declaration of Brunswick which accompanied the invasion of French territory, and she was in particular the author of the famous threat therein contained to give over Paris to military execution, and to hold all the popular authorities responsible with their lives for the restoration of the pre-revolutionary state of affairs.

As research proceeds, the capital effect of this woman's continual and decided interference will be more and more apparent to historians.

Now Marie Antoinette's conception of mankind in general was the conception that you will find prevalent in such societies as that domestic and warm centre which had nourished her childhood. The romantic affection of a few equals, the personal loyalty of a handful of personal servants, the vague histrionic content which permeates the poor at the sight of great equipages and rich accoutrements, the cheers of a crowd when such symbols accompanying monarchy are displayed in the streets—all these were for Marie Antoinette the fundamental political feelings of mankind. An absence of them she regarded with bewilderment, an active opposition to them she hated as something at once incomprehensible and positively evil.

There was in all this illusion, of course, a great element of what the English call middle class, and the French bourgeois. To be quite ignorant of what servitors will say of their masters behind their backs; not to appreciate that heroic devotion is the faculty of a few; never to have imagined the discontents of men in general, and the creative desire for self-expression which inspires men when they act politically; not to know that men as a whole (and particularly the French people) are not deceived by the accidents of wealth, nor attach any real inferiority to poverty; to despise the common will of numbers or to doubt its existence; to see society established in a hierarchy not of office but of leisure: all this may seem to the democrat a very unnatural and despicable mood. But it was not despicable, still less unnatural; in the case of Marie Antoinette: it was the only experience and the only conception of society which had ever been given her. She had always believed, when she gazed upon a mass of the populace, that the difference between the crowd and herself was a moral reality. The contrast in external habits between the wealthy, the middle class, and the poor—a contrast ultimately produced by differences in the opportunity and leisure which wealth affords—she thought to be fundamental. Just as children and certain domestic pet animals regard such economic accidents in society as something real which differentiates men, so did she;—but she happened to nourish this illusion in the midst of a people, and within a day's walk of a capital, where the misconception had less hold than in any other district of Europe.

Of the traits peculiar to the French she knew nothing, or, to put it more strongly, she could not believe that they really existed.

The extremes of cruelty into which this people could fall were inconceivable to her, as were also the extremes of courage to which they can rise under the same excitements as arouse them to an excess of hatred. But that character in the French which she most utterly failed to foresee or to comprehend, was their power of *corporate organisation*.

That a multitude could instruct and order themselves for a common purpose, rapidly acquire and nominate the officers who should bring that purpose to fruition, and in general pass in one moment from a mere multitude to an incipient army—that was a faculty which the French had and have to a peculiar degree, and which she (like so many of our own contemporaries, and especially those of German blood) could not believe to be real. This faculty in the French, when it took action and was apparent in the physical struggles of the Revolution, seemed to her, to the very end, a sort of nightmare; something which, by all the laws of reality, *ought not* to be happening, but somehow or other *was* happening in a manner evilly miraculous. It was her ignorance upon this main point of all that caused her to rely so continually upon the use of the regular forces, and of those forces in insufficient numbers. She could not but believe that a few trained soldiery were necessarily the masters of great civilian bodies; their uniforms were a powerful argument with her, and mere civilian bodies, however numerous, were always, in her conception, a dust of disparate and inchoate humanity. She believed there was nothing to attack or resist in popular numbers but the opinion, the fear, or the cupidity of the individual. In this error of judgment concerning the French people she was not peculiar: it is an error repeated over and over again by foreigners, and even by some native commentators when they seek to account for some national movement of the Gauls. The unlearning of it is the first lesson which those who would either administrate or resist the French should learn.

In the matter of religion (which the reader may see in these pages to be of such moment in the revolutionary story), the queen was originally far more indifferent than her husband, though she observed a certain measure of personal practice. It was not until her heavy misfortunes came upon her that any degree of personal devotion appeared in her daily life, though it must be admitted that, by a sort of premonition of disaster, she turned to religion in the months immediately preceding the outbreak of the reform.

It remains to describe the personal effect she had upon those who were in her immediate presence. Most of the French aristocracy she repelled. The same misfortune which made her unable to understand the French temperament as a whole divorced her from that particular corner of it which took the shape of French aristocratic tradition. She did not understand its stiffness, its exactitude, its brilliancy or its hardness: and she heartily disliked all four.

On this account she produced on the great families of her court, and especially upon the women of them, an effect of vulgarity. Had she survived, and had her misfortunes not been of so tragic an intensity, the legend she would have left in French society would certainly have been one of off-handed carelessness, self-indulgence, and lack of dignity which have for the French of that rank the savour that a loud voice, a bad accent, an insufficient usage in the rules of daily conduct, leave upon what is left of a corresponding rank in England to-day.

She was, on the other hand, easily deceived by the flattery of place seekers, and the great power which she wielded in politics just before the Revolution broke out made her, as it were, a sort of *butt* of the politiciansThey haunted her presence, they depended upon her patronage, and, at the same time, they secretly ridiculed her. Her carriage, which was designed to impress onlookers and did have that effect upon most foreigners, seemed to most of the French observers (of a rank which permitted them to approach her familiarly) somewhat theatrical and sometimes actually absurd. The earnestness which she displayed in several lines of conduct, and notably in her determined animosity to certain characters (as that of La Fayette, for instance), was of an open and violent sort which seemed to them merely brutal and unintelligent; her luxury, moreover, was noticed by the refined world of Versailles to be hardly ever of her own choosing, but nearly always practised in imitation of others.

In connection with that trait of luxury, the reader must appreciate at the outset that it was grievously exaggerated by her contemporaries, and has been still more exaggerated by posterity. She was not a very frivolous, still less a dissipated, woman. She was woefully loose in tongue, but she was certainly virtuous.

She gambled, but as the times went, and the supposed unlimited fortune of the Crown, her gambling was not often excessive; her expenditure upon jewellery and dress would be thought most moderate to-day in the case of any lady of our wealthier families. On the other hand, her whims were continual and as continually changing, especially in the earlier part of her life.

Since that surrounding world of the Court which she misunderstood and which had no sympathy with her was ready to find some handle against her, that handle of dissipation was the easiest for them to seize; but the accusation was not a just one.

Had fortune made her the wife of a poor man in a lower class of society, Marie Antoinette would have been a capable housewife: her abundant energy would have found a proper channel, and she was in no way by nature extravagant.

She had a few very passionate and somewhat too sentimental friendships, some of which were returned, others of which their objects exploited to their own advantage. The two most famous were her friendship for the Princess de Lamballe and for Madame de Polignac. These moved her not infrequently to unwise acts of patronage which were immediately seized by the popular voice and turned against her. They were among the few weaknesses apparent in her general temper. They were certainly ill balanced and ill judged.

She indulged also in a number of small and unimportant flirtations which might almost be called the routine of her rank and world; she had but one great affection in her life for the other sex, and it was most ardently returned. Its object was a Swedish noble of her own age, the very opposite of the French in his temper, romantically chivalrous, unpractical in the extreme, gentle, intensely reserved; his name Count Axel de Fersen. The affair remained pure, but she loved him with her whole heart, and in the last months of her tragedy this emotion must be regarded as the chief concern of her soul. They saw each other but very rarely, often they were separated for years; it was this, perhaps, which lent both glamour and fidelity to the strange romance.

MIRABEAU

Mirabeau, the chief of the "practical" men of the Revolution (as the English language would render the most salient point in their political attitude), needs a very particular examination. His influence upon the early part of the Revolution was so considerable, the effect of his death was so determinant and final, the speculation as to what *might* have happened had he survived is so fruitful, so entertaining, and so common, and the positive effect of his attitude upon the development of the Revolution after his death was so wide, that to misunderstand Mirabeau is in a large measure to misunderstand the whole movement; and Mirabeau has unfortunately been ill or superficially understood by many among now three generations of historians; for a comprehension of this character is not a matter for research nor for accumulated historic detail, but rather a task for sympathy.

Mirabeau was essentially an artist, with the powers and the frailties which we properly associate with that term: that is, strong emotion appealed to him both internally and externally. He loved to enjoy it himself, he loved to create it in others. He studied, therefore, and was a master of, the material by which such emotion may be created; he himself yielded to strong emotion and sought it where it might be found. It is foolish alike to belittle and to exaggerate this type of temperament. Upon it or upon its admixture with other qualities is based the music, the plastic art, and in a large measure the permanent literature of the world. This aptitude for the enjoyment and for the creation in others of emotion clothes intellectual work in a manner which makes it permanent. This is what we mean when we say that *style* is necessary to a book; that a great civilisation may partly be judged by its architecture; that, as Plato says, music may be moral or immoral, and so forth. The artist, though he is not at the root of human affairs, is a necessary and proper ally in their development.

When I say that Mirabeau was an artist I mean that wherever his energies might have found play he would there have desired to enjoy and to create enjoyment through some definite medium. This medium was in part literary, but much more largely oral expression. To be a *tribune*, that is the voice of great numbers, to persuade, nay, to please by his very accents and the very rhythm of his sentences, these things occupied the man; but he also brought into his art that without which no great art can exist: mere intellect.

He believed in the main principles at least which underlay the revolutionary movement, he understood them and he was prepared to propagate them; but his power over men was not due to this conviction: his power over men was wholly that of the artist, and had he by some accident been engaged in maintaining the attack against democracy, he would have been nearly as famous as he became under the title of its defender. We must then always consider Mirabeau as an orator, though an orator endowed with a fine and clear intelligence and with no small measure of reasoned faith.

Much else remains to be said of him.

He was a gentleman; that is, he both enjoyed and suffered the consequences which attach to hereditary wealth and to the atmosphere that surrounds its expenditure. On this account, he being personally insufficiently provided with wealth, he was for ever in debt, and regarded the sums necessary to his station in life and to his large opportunities as things due to him, so to speak, from society. We are right when we say that he took bribes, but wrong if we imagine that those bribes bound him as they would bind a man meaner in character or less lucky in his birth. He stooped as gentlemen will to all manner of low intrigues, to obtain "the necessary and the wherewith"; that is, money for his *rôle*. But there was a driving power behind him, bound up with his whole character, which made it impossible for any such sums to control his diction or to make of such a man a mere advocate. He was never that dirtiest of political phenomena, the "party man." He would never have been, had he been born a hundred years later and thrust into the nastiness of modern parliamentary life, "a parliamentary hand."

Mirabeau had behind him a certain personal history which we must read in connection with his temperament.

He had travelled widely, he knew Englishmen and Germans of the wealthier classes well. The populace he knew ill even in his own country; abroad he knew it not at all. He had suffered from his father's dislike of him, from the consequence of his own unbridled passions, also not a little from mere accidental misfortune. Capable of prolonged and faithful attachment to some woman, the opportunity for that attachment had never been afforded him until the last few months before his death. Capable of paying loyal and industrious service to some political system, no political system had chosen him for its servant. It is a fruitful matter of speculation to consider what he might have done for the French monarchy had Fate put him early at Court and given him some voice in the affairs of the French Executive before the Revolution broke out. As it was, the Revolution provided him with his opportunity merely because it broke down old barriers and conventions and was destructive of the framework of the State in which he lived. He was compelled to enter the Revolution as something of a destroyer, for by no other avenue could he be given his chance; but by nature he detested destruction. I mean (since this phrase is somewhat vague) he detested that spirit which will disendow a nation of certain permanent institutions serving definite ends, without a clear scheme of how those institutions should be replaced by others to serve similar ends. It was on this account that he was most genuinely and sincerely a defender of the monarchy: a permanent institution serving the definite ends of national unity and the repression of tendencies to oligarchy in the State.

Mirabeau had none of the revolutionary Vision. In mind he was prematurely aged, for his mind had worked very rapidly over a very varied field of experience. The pure doctrine of democracy which was a religion to many of his contemporaries, with all the consequences of a religion, he had never thought of accepting. But certain consequences of the proposed reforms strongly appealed to him. He loved to be rid of meaningless and dead barriers, privileges which no longer corresponded to real social differences, old traditions in the management of trade which no longer corresponded to the economic circumstances of his time, and (this is the pivotal point) the fossils of an old religious creed which, like nearly all of his rank, he simply took for granted to be dead: for Mirabeau was utterly divorced from the Catholic Church.

Much has been said and will be said in these pages concerning the religious quarrel which, though men hardly knew it at the time, cut right across the revolutionary effort, and was destined to form the lasting line of cleavage in French life. There will be repeated again and again what has already been written, that a reconciliation between the Catholic Church and the reconstruction of democracy was, though men did not know it, the chief temporal business of the time, and the reader of these pages will be made well acquainted in them with the degradation to which religion had fallen among the cultivated of that generation. But in the case of Mirabeau this absence of religion must be particularly insisted upon. It would no more have occurred to Mirabeau that the Catholic Faith had a future than it could occur to (let us say) an English politician of thirty years ago that the Irish might become a wealthy community or that an English Government might within his own lifetime find itself embarrassed for money. I use this parallel for the sake of strengthening my contention, but it is indeed a weak parallel. No contemporary parallel in our strange and rapidly changing times corresponds to the fixed certitude which permeated the whole of the end of the eighteenth century that the Catholic Faith was dead. Mirabeau had perhaps never engaged in his life in intimate conversation a single man who took the Catholic sacraments seriously, or suffered a moment's anxiety upon the tenets of the creed.

He knew, indeed, that certain women and a much smaller number of insignificant men wrapped themselves up in old practices of an odd, superstitious kind; he knew that great, dull areas of ignorant peasantry, in proportion to their poverty and isolation, repeated by rote the old formulae of the Faith. But of the Faith as a living thing he could have no conception.

He saw on the one hand a clerical institution, economic in character, providing places and revenues for men of his own rank; he met those men and never discovered them to have any religion at all. He saw on the other hand a proposed society in which such a fossil, unjust and meaningless, must relinquish its grip upon those large revenues. But of the Faith as a social force, as a thing able to revive, he could have no conception. It would have seemed to him a mere folly to suggest that the future might contain the possibility of such a resurrection. The dissolution of the religious orders, which was largely his work, the civil constitution of the clergy which he presided over, were to him the most natural acts in the world. They were the mere sweeping away of a quantity of inorganic stuff which cumbered the modern State. He felt of them as we might feel of the purchase of waste spaces in our cities, of the confiscation of some bad landlords' property in them. The Church served no kind of purpose, no one who counted believed in it, it was defended only by people who enjoyed large revenues from the survival of what had once been, but was now no longer, a living, social function.

In everything of the Revolution which he understood Mirabeau was upon the side of caution. He was not oblivious to the conception of popular government, he was not even mistrustful of it, but he could not conceive of it save as acting through the established strength of the wealthier classes. Of military power he judged very largely through Prussian eyes. And in long and enthusiastic passages he described the Prussian army as invincible. Had he lived to see the military enthusiasm of the Republicans he would utterly have distrusted it. He favoured in his heart an aristocratic machinery of society—though not an aristocratic theory of the State; he was quite determined to preserve as a living but diminished national organ the traditional monarchy of France; he was curious upon a number of details which were present and close to his eyes: methods of voting, constitutional checks, commercial codes and the rest of it. The little equilibriums of diplomacy interested him also, and the watching of men immediately under his eye in the Parliament.

It was in the Parliament that his whole activity lay, it was there that he began to guide the Revolution, it was his absence from the Parliament after his death that the Revolution most feels in the summer of 1791.

This very brief sketch does not present Mirabeau to the reader. He can only be properly presented in his speeches and in the more rhetorical of his documents. It is probable as time proceeds that his reputation in this department will grow. His constitutional ideas, based as they were upon foreign institutions, and especially upon the English of that time, were not applicable to his own people and are now nearly forgotten: he was wrong upon English politics as he was wrong upon the German armies, but he had art over men and his personality endures and increases with time.

LA FAYETTE

The character of La Fayette has suffered chiefly from his own aloofness towards his contemporaries on the one hand, and from his rigid adherence to principle upon the other. Both these causes are clearly connected. The same quality in him which made him so tenacious of principle made him contemptuous of the run of men about him. Fundamentally, he was nearer the extreme Republicans than any other class, from the very fact of his possessing a clear political creed and a determination to follow it out to its logical consequence. But there was no chance of his comprehending the concrete side of the movement or the men engaged upon it, for his great wealth, inherited in very early life, had cut him off from experience. His moral fault was undoubtedly ambition. It was an ambition which worked in the void, as it were, and never measured itself with other men's capacities or opportunities. He made no plans for advancement, not because he would have despised the use of intrigue in reason, but because he was incapable of working it. He was exceedingly attached to popularity, when it came he thought it his due; unpopularity in its turn seemed to him a proof of the vileness of those who despised him. He made himself too much the measure of his world.

Undoubtedly a very great part in the moulding of his character proceeded from his experience in the United States of America. He was then at the most impressionable and formative period of human life, little more than a boy, or at least just entering early manhood. He had just married, he had just come into the administration of his vast fortune. At such a moment he took part in the victorious rebellion of the English colonies, and it may be imagined how powerful was the effect of this youthful vision upon the whole of the man's future life; because there was no proletariat in the colonies, he never saw or comprehended the dispossessed classes of Paris—for that matter he never saw or comprehended the French peasantry upon his own lands; because a chance and volunteer soldiery had, under the peculiar conditions of the half-populated Atlantic seaboard in conjunction with the French fleet and with the aid of French money and arms, got the better of the small and heterogeneous forces of George III, he believed that a military nation like the French, in the midst of powerful enemies, could make something of an amateur civic force; because a certain type of ease in social relations was the ideal of many, perhaps of most, of those with whom he had served in America, he confused so simple and mundane an ideal with the fierce crusading blast and the sacred passion for equality which was stirring his own nation when his opportunity for leadership came.

It may be said of La Fayette with justice that he never upon a single occasion did the right thing. It may also be said with justice that he never did politically any major thing for which his own conscience would later reproach him. It is noticeable that the Queen held him in particular odium. He had been a wealthy young noble about the Court, the friend of all her women friends, and his sympathy with the revolutionary movement at its inception therefore seemed to her nothing better than treason. There was also undoubtedly something in his manner which grievously repelled her; that it was self-sufficient we cannot doubt, and that it was often futile and therefore exasperating to women, events are sufficient to show. But Marie Antoinette's violent personal antagonism towards La Fayette was not common, though several ardent spirits (Danton's, for instance) shared it. The mass of those who came across La Fayette felt in connection with him a certain irritation or a certain contempt or a certain rather small and distant respect; he inspired no enthusiasms, and when he timidly attempted a rebellion against the new Government after the fall of the monarchy, no one would sacrifice himself or follow him.

It may be affirmed of La Fayette that if he had not existed the Revolution would have pursued much the same course as it did, with this exception: that there would not have been formed a definitely middle class armed guard to provoke friction in Paris: the National Guard would have been more open to all ranks.

In religion the man was anodyne, Catholic of course by baptism, but distinctly Protestant in morals and in general tone, in dogma (until the end of his life) freethinking, of course, like all his contemporaries. He was personally courageous but foolishly despised the duel. One anecdote out of many will help to fix his nature in the mind of the reader. Mirabeau, casting about as usual for aid in his indebtedness, sent urgently to him as to a fellow noble, a fellow politician and a fellow supporter of the Crown, begging a loan of £2000. La Fayette accorded him £1000.

DUMOURIEZ

Dumouriez presents a character particularly difficult for the modern Englishman to comprehend, so remote is it in circumstance and fundamentals from those of our time.

Of good birth, but born in a generation when social differences had become a jest for intelligent and active men (and he was intelligent and active), courageous, with a good knowledge of his trade of soldiering, of rapid decision and excellent judgment where troops or *terrain* were concerned, he was all at sea in the comprehension of men, and he bore no loyalty to the StatIt is this last feature which will particularly surprise the English reader, for it is the singular and permanent advantage of oligarchic communities such as the British that they retain under any stress and show throughout the whole commonwealth the sense of the State. To betray the State, to act against its interests, to be imperfectly conscious of its existence, are crimes or weaknesses unknown to the citizens of an oligarchy, and a citizen of this country cannot easily conceive of them to-day. In democracies and despotisms, on the other hand, to forget one's duty to the State, to be almost oblivious of its corporate existence, is a common weakness. There is here a compensation, and by just so much as despotism and democracy permit rapid, effective and all-compelling action on the part of the State, by just so much as they permit sudden and sometimes miraculous enthusiasms which save or which confirm a State, by that also do they lack the quiet and persistent consciousness of the State which oligarchy fosters and determines.

Dumouriez' excellence as a general can only be appreciated by those who have looked closely into the constitution of the forces which he was to command and the adversaries with whom he had to deal. It is the prime quality of a great commander that his mind stands ready for any change in circumstances or in the material to his hand, and even when we have allowed for the element of luck which is so considerable in military affairs, we must not forget that Dumouriez saved without disaster the wretched and disorganised bands, inchoate and largely mutinous as to their old units, worthless and amateur as to their new, which had to meet, in and behind the Argonne, the model army of Prussia.

We must not forget that his plan for the invasion of the Low Countries was a just and sensible one, nor with what skill, after the inevitable defeat and retreat of the spring of 1793, he saved his command intact.

As a subordinate to an armed executive, to the Government of Napoleon, for instance, the man would have been priceless. Nay, had circumstances permitted him to retain supreme command of civil as of military power, he would have made no bad dictator. His mere technical skill was so considerable as to make the large sums paid him by the English Government seem a good bargain even at our distance of time, and his plans for the defence of England and for the attack on Napoleon are a proof of the value at which he was estimated.

But Dumouriez was quite unable to act under the special circumstances in which he happened to be placed at the moment of his treason. A mere ambition had carried him from intrigue to intrigue among the politicians. He despised them as an active and capable soldier was compelled to despise them; he was too old to share any of their enthusiasms, even had his temperament permitted him to entertain any vision, political or religious. He certainly never felt the least moral bond attaching him to what was in his eyes the chance anarchy of the last six months of French Government under which he served, and if he is to be branded with the title of traitor, then we must brand with the same title all that multitude of varied men who escaped from the country in the Emigration, who left it in disgust, or even who remained in France, but despaired of French fortunes, in the turmoil of 1793.

It is perhaps a worthy excuse for Dumouriez' failure to point out that he also was one of those whom the Court might have used had it known how to use men; but the Court had no such knowledge.

DANTON

The character of Danton has more widely impressed the world than that of any other revolutionary leader, because it contained elements permanently human, independent of the democratic theory of the time, and necessary neither to the support of that theory nor to the criticism of it.

The character of Danton appeals to that sense in man which is interested in action, and which in the field of letters takes the form of drama. His vigour, his personal strength of mind and body, the individuality of his outline, arrest equally the man who loves the Revolution, and the man who hates it, and the man who is quite indifferent to its success or failure.

It is on this very account that historians, especially foreign historians, have tended to misinterpret the man. Thus Carlyle, who has great intuition in the matter, yet makes him out farmer-like—which he certainly was not; Michelet, fascinated by his energy, presents him as something uncouth, and in general those who would describe Danton stand at a distance, as it were, where his loud voice and forcible gesture may best be appreciated; but a man to be seen truly must be seen in intimacy.

Danton was essentially a compound of two powerful characters in man. He was amative or constructive, and at the same time he not only possessed but liked to exercise lucidity of thought. The combination is among the strongest of all those that go to build up human personalities.

That which was amative and constructive in him, his virility if you will, brought him into close touch with reality; he knew and loved his own country, for instance, and infinitely preferred its happy survival to the full development of any political theory. He also knew and loved his fellow countrymen in detail and as persons; he knew what made a Frenchman weak and what made him strong. The vein of Huguenotry, though he did not know it for what it was, he disliked in his compatriots. On the other hand, the salt and freshness of the French was native to him and he delighted in it; the freedom of their expression, the noise of their rhetoric, and the military subsoil of them, were things to all of which he immediately responded. He understood their sort of laughter, nor was he shocked, as a man less national would have been, at their peculiarly national vices, and in especial their lapses into rage. It is this which must account for what all impartial judgment most blames in him, which is, his indifference to the cruelties, his absorbed interest in foreign and military affairs, at the moment of the Massacres of September.

This touch with reality made him understand in some fashion (though only from without) the nature of the Germans. The foolish mania of their rulers for mere territorial expansion unaccompanied by persuasion or the spread of their ideas, he comprehended. The vast superiority of their armies over the disorganised forces of the French in 1792 he clearly seized: hence on the one hand his grasp of their foreign policy, and on the other his able negotiation of the retreat after Valmy. He also understood, however, and more profoundly, the rapid self-organisation of which his own countrymen were capable, and it was upon this knowledge that his determination to risk the continuance of the war reposed. It should be remarked that both in his military and in his quasi-military action he was himself endowed in a singular degree with that power of immediate decision which is characteristic of his nation.

His lucidity of thought permitted him to foresee the consequences of many a revolutionary decision, and at the same time inclined him to a strong sympathy with the democratic creed, with the doctrine of equality, and especially with the remoulding of the national institutions—particularly his own profession of the law—upon simple lines. He was undoubtedly a sincere and a convinced revolutionary, and one whose doctrine more permeated him than did that of many of his contemporaries their less solid minds. He was not on that account necessarily republican. Had some accident called his genius into play earlier in the development of the struggle, he might well, like Mirabeau, with whom he presents so curious a parallel, have thought it better for the country to save the Monarchy.

It must always be remembered that he was a man of wide culture and one who had achieved an early and satisfactory professional success; he was earning a sound income at the moment of his youthful marriage; he read English largely and could speak it. His dress was not inexpensive, and though somewhat disordered (as it often is with men of intense energy and constant gesture) it never gave an impression of carelessness or disarray. He had many and indifferent intellectual interests, and was capable, therefore, of intelligent application in several fields. He appreciated the rapid growth of physical science, and at the same time the complexity of the old social conditions—too widely different from contemporary truths.

To religion he was, of course, like all men of that time, utterly indifferent, but unlike many of them he seized the precise proportion of its remaining effect upon certain districts and certain sections of the countrysides. There has been a tendency latterly to exaggerate the part which Freemasonry played in the launching of him; he was indeed a member of a masonic lodge, as were, for that matter, all the men, conspicuous or obscure, democratic or utterly reactionary, who appeared upon the revolutionary stage: probably the king, certainly old aristocrats like the father of Madame de Lamballe, and the whole host of the middle class, from men like Bailly to men like Condorcet. But it is reading history backwards, and imagining the features of our own time to have been present a century ago, to make of Masonry the determining element in his career.

Danton failed and died from two combined causes: first his health gave way, secondly he obtruded his sanity and civilian sense into the heated fury and calculated martial law of the second year of the Republic. To both that fury and that calculation he was an obstacle; his opposition to the Terror lost him the support of the enthusiasts, but it was the interference which such a judgment made in the plans of the soldiers, and notably of Carnot, that determined his condemnation and death. He also, like Mirabeau, will undoubtedly increase as the years proceed, and, if only as a representative of the national temper, become more and more the typical figure of the Revolution in action.

CARNOT

Carnot, the predecessor of Napoleon, and the organising soldier of the early revolutionary wars, owed his power to backbone.

He had not only a good solidity of brain, but an astonishing power of using it for hours and hours on end. This he owed perhaps to the excellent physical stock of which he came, the eldest of a very large family born to a notable lawyer in Burgundy.

It was Carnot's pride to hold a commission in the learned arms which were to transform at that moment the art of war: for as Bonaparte, his successor, was a gunner, so he was a sapper. His practice of exact knowledge in application, and the liberal education which his career demanded, further strengthened the strong character he had inherited. More important still, in his democratic views he was what none of the older officers had been, convinced and sincere. He had not come within the influence of the very wealthy or of the very powerful. He was young, and he knew his own mind not only in matters of political faith but in the general domain of philosophy, and in the particular one of military science.

It has been said of him that he invented the revolutionary method of strategical concentration and tactical massing in the field. There is some truth in this; but the method would not have been possible had he not also invented, in company with Danton, and supported after Danton left power, a universal system of conscription.

Carnot understood, as only trained soldiers can, the value of numbers, and *he depended with great sagacity upon the national temper*; thus at Wattignies, which was a victory directly due to his genius, though it was novel in him to have massed troops suddenly upon the right after a check on the extreme left of the field, yet the novelty would have been of no effect had he not comprehended that, with his young fellow countrymen as troopers, he could depend upon a charge delivered after thirty-six hours of vigil.

He used not only the national but also the revolutionary temper in war. One of the chief features, for instance, of the revolutionary armies when they began to be successful, was the development of lines of skirmishers who pushed out hardily before the main bodies and were the first in the history of modern warfare to learn the use of cover. This development was spontaneous: it was produced within and by each unit, not by any general command. But Carnot recognised it at Hoondschoote and used it ever after.

The stoical inflexibility of his temper is the noblest among the many noble characters of his soul. He never admitted the empire, and he suffered exile, seeming thereby in the eyes of the vilest and most intelligent of his contemporaries, Fouché, to be a mere fool. He was as hard with himself as with others, wholly military in the framework of his mind, and the chief controller of the Terror, which he used, as it was intended to be used, for the military salvation of the republic.

MARAT

Marat is easily judged. The complete sincerity of the enthusiast is not difficult to appreciate when his enthusiasm is devoted to a simple human ideal which has been, as it were, fundamental and common to the human race.

Equality within the State and the government of the State by its general will: these primal dogmas, on the reversion to which the whole Revolution turned, were Marat's creed.

Those who would ridicule or condemn him because he held such a creed, are manifestly incapable of discussing the matter at all. The ridicule and condemnation under which Marat justly falls do not attach to the patent moral truths he held, but to the manner in which he held them. He did not only hold them isolated from other truths—it is the fault of the fanatic so to hold any truth—but he held them as though no other truths existed. And whenever he found his ideal to be in practice working at a friction or stopped dead, his unnourished and acute enthusiasms at once sought a scapegoat, discovered a responsible agent, and suggested a violent outlet, for the delay.

He was often right when he denounced a political intriguer: he often would have sacrificed a victim not unjustly condemned, he often discovered an agent partially responsible, and even the violent solutions that he suggested were not always impracticable. But it was the prime error of his tortured mind that beyond victims, and sudden violent clutches at the success of democracy, there was nothing else he could conceive. He was incapable of allowing for imperfections, for stupidities, for the misapprehension of mind by mind, for the mere action of time, and for all that renders human life infinitely complex and infinitely adjustable.

Humour, the reflection of such wisdom, he lacked;—"judgment" (as the English idiom has it) he lacked still more—if a comparative term may be attached to two such absolute vacuities.

It must not be forgotten that so complete an absence of certain necessary qualities in the building up of a mind are equivalent to madness. Marat was not sane. His insanity was often generous, the creed to which it was attached was obvious enough, and in the eyes of most of us it is a creed to be accepted. But he worked with it as a madman who is mad on collectivism, let us say, or the rights of property, might work in our society, thinking of his one thesis, shrieking it and foaming at the mouth upon it, losing all control when its acceptance was not even opposed but merely delayed. He was valueless for the accomplishment of the ends of the Revolution. His doctrine and his adherence to it were so conspicuously simple and sincere that it is no wonder the populace made him (for a few months) a sort of symbol of their demand.

For the rest, his face, like his character, was tortured; he carried with him a disease of the skin that irritated perpetually his wholly unbalanced temper.

Some say (but one must always beware of so-called "Science" in the reading of history) that a mixture of racial types produced in him a perpetual physical disturbance: his face was certainly distorted and ill-balanced—but physical suggestions of that sort are very untrustworthy.

Those who met him in the management of affairs thought him worthless enough; a few who knew him intimately loved him dearly; more who came across him continually were fatigued and irritated by his empty violence. He was, among those young revolutionaries, almost an elderly man; he was (this should never be forgotten) a distinguished scholar in his own trade, that of medicine; and he effected less in the Revolution than any man to whom a reputation of equal prominence happened to attach. He must stand responsible for the massacres of September.*

ROBESPIERRE

No character in the Revolution needs for its comprehension a wider reading and a greater knowledge of the national character than Robespierre's.

Upon no character does the comprehension of the period more depend, and none (for reasons I will give in a moment) has been more misunderstood, not only in the popular legend but in the weighed decisions of competent historians.

So true is this that even time, which (in company with scholarship) usually redresses such errors, has not yet permitted modern authors to give a true picture of the man.

The reason of so conspicuous a failure in the domain of history is this: that side by side with the real Robespierre there existed in the minds of all his contemporaries *save those who actually came across him in the junctions of government*, a legendary Robespierre—a Robespierre popularly imagined; and that this imaginary Robespierre, while it (or he) has proved odious to posterity, seemed, while he lived, a fascinating portrait to the man himself, and therefore he accepted it. For Robespierre, though just, lacked humility.

The problem is an exceedingly subtle as well as an exceedingly difficult one. The historian, as he reads his authorities, has perpetually to distinguish between what is strong and what is weak evidence, and to recall himself, as he reads, to reality by a recollection of what Robespi-

---

* There is but one trustworthy monograph on Marat. It will interest the student as a proof of the enthusiasm which Marat can inspire. It is by Chèvremont.

erre himself was. If he does not do so he falls at once into the legend; so powerful is that legend in the numbers that supported it, and so strongly did Robespierre himself support it by his own attitude. The legendary Robespierre may be described in a very few lines.

Conceive a man sincerely convinced of the purest democratic theory, a man who cared for nothing else but the realisation of that theory, and who had never sacrificed his pursuit of its realisation in the State to any personal advantage whatsoever. This man, trusted by the people and at last idolised by them, becomes more and more powerful. He enters the governing body (the Committee of Public Safety), he is the master both within and without that body, and uses his mastery for establishing an ideal democracy which shall recognise the existence of God and repose upon civic virtue; and to establish this ideal he has recourse to terror. He finds that human defections from his ideal are increasingly numerous: he punishes them by death. The slaughter grows to be enormous; the best of Democrats are involved in it; at last it can be tolerated no longer, his immediate subordinates revolt against him in the Committee, he is outlawed, fails to raise a popular rebellion in his favour in Paris, is executed, and his system of terror falls to the ground.

This picture, though purely legendary in tone, contains not only much truth, but truth of precisely that sort which conspires to make credible what is false in the whole.

Robespierre was sincerely attached to the conception of an ideal democracy; he was incorruptible in the pursuit of it—and to be a politician and incorruptible amounts to something like what the Church calls heroic virtue in a man. He *did* enter the Committee of Public Safety; he *did* support the Terror, and when he was overthrown the Terror *did* come to an end. Where, then, does the legend differ from the truth?

In these capital points, which change it altogether: that Robespierre was not the chief influence in the Committee of Public Safety, *i.e.* the all powerful executive of the Republic; that he did not desire the Terror, that he did not use it, that he even grew disgusted with it, and that, in general, he was never the man who governed FraIt need hardly be pointed out how such a truth destroys such a legend. The whole nature of the twelve months between the summer of 1793 and the summer of 1794 must vary according as we regard them as Robespierrean or no: and they were not Robespierrean.

What were they then, and why has the error that Robespierre was then master, arisen?

Those months, which may be roughly called the months of the Terror, were, as we shall see later in this book, months of martial law; and the Terror was simply martial law in action—a method of enforcing the military defence of the country and of punishing all those who interfered with it or were supposed by the Committee to interfere with it.

No one man in the Committee was the author of this system, but the one most determined to use it and the one who had most occasion to use it, was undoubtedly the military organiser, Carnot. Side by side with him one man, such as Barrère, supported it because it kept up the Committee of Public Safety which gave him all his political position. Another, such as Saint-Just, supported it because he believed that the winning of the war (in which he took an active part) would secure democracy everywhere and for ever. Another, such as Jean Bon, supported it from the old sectarian bitterness of the Huguenot. But of all men in the Committee, Robespierre supported the Terror least, and was most suspected by his colleagues—and increasingly suspected as time went on—of desiring to interfere with the martial system of the Terror and to modify it.

Why, then, was Robespierre popularly identified with the Terror, and why, when he was executed, did the Terror cease?

Robespierre was identified with the Terror because he was identified with the popular clamour of the time, with the extreme democratic feeling of the time, and its extreme fear of a reaction. Robespierre being the popular idol, had become also the symbol of a popular frenzy which was supposed to be ruling the country. But that frenzy was not ruling the country. What was ruling the country was the Committee of Public Safety, in which Carnot's was the chief brain. Robespierre was indeed the idol of the populace; he was in no way the agent of their power or of any power.

Why, when he fell, did the Terror cease if he were not its author? Because the Terror was acting under a strain; it was with the utmost difficulty that this absolute, intolerant and intolerable martial system could be continued when once the fear of invasion was removed. For some weeks before Robespierre fell the victories had begun to render it unnecessary. When the Committee saw to it that Robespierre should be outlawed by the Parliament, they knocked away, without knowing it, the keystone of their own policy; it was *his* popular position which made *their* policy possible. When he was destroyed they suddenly found that the Terror could no longer be maintained. Men had borne with it because of Robespierre, falsely imagining that Robespierre had desired it. Robespierre gone, men would not bear with it any more.

Now, finally, if Robespierre himself had always felt opposed to the system of the Terror, why did he not take the lead in the popular reaction against it?

He had his opportunity given him by Danton in December 1793— seven months before his own catastrophe. The Committee determined to put Danton out of the way because Danton, in appealing for mercy, was weakening the martial power of their government. Robespierre might have saved Danton: he preferred to let him be sacrificed. The reason was that Robespierre wrongly believed popularity to lie upon the side of the Terror and against Danton; he was in no way a leader (save in rhetoric and in rhetoric directed towards what men already desired), and his own great weakness or vice was the love of popular acclaim.

Later on, in the summer of 1794, when he actually began to move against the Terror, he only did so privately. He so misread men that he still believed the Terror to be popular, and dared not lose his popular name. A man by nature as sincere as crystal, he was tempted to insincerity in this major thing, during the last months of his life, and he yielded completely to the temptation. For the sake of his memory it was deplorable, and deplorable also for history. His weakness has been the cause of an historical error as grave as any that can be discovered in modern letters, and at the same time has wholly maligned him to posterity.

A factor in Robespierre's great public position which is often forgotten is the great effect of his speeches. That men should still debate, after so vast a change in taste, whether those speeches were eloquent or no, is a sufficient proof of their effect. He spoke in an ordered and a reasoned manner, which bored the fine spirits of the earlier Parliaments, but well suited the violent convictions of the later Revolution. His phraseology, his point of view, just jumped with that of his audience. He could express what they felt, and express it in terms which they knew to be exact, and which they believed to be grand. For his manner was never excessive, and those excessive men who heard him in an excessive mood, were proud to know that their violence could be expressed with so much scholarship and moderated skill.

By birth he was of the smaller gentry, though poor. It is an indication of his character that he had thought of taking Orders, and that in early youth literary vanity had affected him. He has left no monument; but from the intensity of his faith and from his practice of it, his name, though it will hardly increase, will certainly endure.

CHAPTER IV

THE PHASES OF THE REVOLUTION

I

From May 1789 to 17th of July 1789.

The first point which the reader must hold in the story of the Revolution is the quarrel between its first Parliament and the Crown.

Of what nature was that quarrel?

It was not, as it has sometimes been represented, a simple issue between privilege and a democratic demand for equality, or between traditional organs of government and a democratic demand for self-government by the nation. To imagine this is to read history backwards, and to see in the untried conditions of 1789 the matured results which only appeared after years of struggle.

The prime issue lay between legality and illegality.

The forms of French law and all the inherited method of French administration demanded a certain form of authority; a centralised government of unlimited power. The King was absolute. From him proceeded in the simplest fashion whatever will was paramount in the State. He could suspend a debtor's liabilities, imprison a man without trial, release him without revision of his case, make war or peace, and in minor details such as the discipline and administration of public bodies, the power of the Crown was theoretically and legally equally supreme. It was not exercised as the enormous power of modern government is exercised, it did not perpetually enter into every detail of the life of the poor in the way in which the power of a modern English Government enters into it; it is in the very nature of such autocratic power that, while unlimited in theory, it is compelled to an instinctive and perpetual self-limitation lest it break down; and autocracy maybe compared in this to aristocracy, or more properly

54

speaking to oligarchy, the government of a few: for where a few govern they know that their government reposes upon public opinion or public tolerance; they are very careful not to exceed certain limits the transgression of which would weaken the moral foundation of their power; they welcome allies, they recruit themselves perpetually from other classes in the community.

In the same way an autocracy always has the desire to be popular. Its strokes affect the great and the powerful, and are hardly ever aimed at the mass of the community. The intellectual, the wealthy, the privileged by birth, fortune or exceptional personal powers, are suspect to it. As for the mass of men an Autocracy attempts to represent and, in a certain sense, to obey them.

Now the French autocracy (for it was no less) erred not in the will to act thus popularly in the early part of the Revolution, but in the *knowledge* requisite for such action.

The Parliament, shortly after it had met in May 1789, began to show, in the Commons part of it, the working of that great theory which had leavened all France for a generation. The Commons said, "We are the people; at once the symbols of the people, the direct mandatory servants of the people, and" (though this was a fiction) "we are of the people in our birth and origin. We are therefore the true sovereign; and the prince, the head of the Executive, is no more than an organ of government, morally less in authority than ourselves, who are the true source of government." This attitude, which was at the back of all men's minds, and which was concentrated, of course, in the Commons, clashed with legality. It could not express itself in the terms of law, it could not act save in a fashion which should be, in the strictest sense of the word, *revolutionary*.

Now the Crown, on the whole national in sympathy, and comprehending this new theory well (I mean by the Crown the general body of advisers round the King, and the King himself), was offended at the illegality not of the theory or of the pretence (for these were not illegal), but of the action of the Commons. And this comparatively small source of friction was the irritant upon which we must fix as the cause of what followed. The Nobles, by 108 to 47, decided, the day after the opening of the Parliament, to sit as a separate House. The Clergy, by a much smaller majority, 133 to 114, came to the same decision, but carefully qualified it as provisional. The Commons declared that the hall in which they met should be regarded as the hall of the National

Assembly, and later made it their business (to quote the phrase of the motion) "to attempt to unite in common all the deputies of the nation in that hall and never to abandon the principle of voting individually" (that is, not by separate Houses) "or the principle that the States-General formed one undivided body." This attitude was qualified and compromised with to some extent in the days that followed, but it held the field, and while the Commons were insisting upon this attitude as a moral right, the Nobles countered by a reaffirmation of the right of each House to a separate judgment upon public matters. The Nobles were standing upon legal precedent: the Commons had nothing in their favour but political theory; if the orders sat all together and voted as individuals, the Commons, who were in number equal to the two other Houses combined, would, with their noble and clerical sympathisers, have a majority.

Now the King and his advisers, notably Necker, who still had great weight, were by no means "Impossiblists" in this struggle. They desired an understanding, and through the last days of May and the first days of June the attempt at an understanding was made. But the attempt dragged, and as it seemed that nothing would come of it, on the 10th of June Sièyes moved that the Assembly should "verify its powers" (a French phrase for admitting and registering the presence of each member as acceptable to the whole body, and to the theory of its Constitution), and that this should be done "in the case of each member" (meaning members of all the three orders and *not* of the Commons alone), "whether the members of the two privileged Houses were present or absent." The roll was called and completed upon the 15th. None of the nobles attended the common roll-call, three of the parish clergy (they were from the province of Poitou) did so, and thus admitted the right of the Commons so to act. A dozen of their colleagues joined them later; but that was all.

So far there had been no action which could be precisely called illegal or revolutionary. The Commons had affirmed a right based upon a political theory which the vast majority of the nation admitted, and the legal depositary of power, the King, had not yet reproved. One may draw a parallel and compare the action of the Commons so far to some action which a trade union, for instance, may take in England; some action the legality of which is doubtful but upon which the courts have not yet decided.

It was upon the 17th of June, two days after the completion of the roll-call by the Commons, that the first revolutionary act took place, and the student of the Revolution will do well to put his finger upon that date and to regard it not indeed as the moral origin of the movement, but as the precise moment from which the Revolution, as a Revolution, begins to act. For upon that day the Commons, though in fact only joined by a handful of the Clerical House, and by none of the nobility, *declared themselves to be the National Assembly*; that is, asserted the fiction that Clergy, Nobles and Commons were all present and voted together. To this declaration they added a definite act of sovereignty which trespassed upon and contradicted the legal authority of the Crown. True, the motion was only moved and passed "provisionally," but the words used were final, for in this motion the self-styled "National Assembly" declared that "provisionally" taxes and dues might be raised upon the old authority but that only until the National Assembly should disperse; "after which day"—and here we reach the sacramental formula, as it were, of the crisis—"the National Assembly *wills and decrees* that all taxes and dues of whatever nature which have not been specifically formally and freely granted by the said Assembly shall cease in every province of the kingdom no matter how such that province may be administered." (This is an allusion to the fact that in some provinces there was a representative machinery, in others nothing but the direct action of the Crown.) "The Assembly declares that when it has *in concert with* (not in obedience to) the King laid down the principle of a national re-settlement, it will busy itself with the examination and ordering of the public debt." Etc., etc.

Such was the point of departure after which sovereignty was at issue between the Crown and the States-General; the Crown a known institution with its traditions stretching back to the Roman Empire, and the National Assembly a wholly new organ according to its own claims, basing its authority upon a political theory stretching back to the very origins of human society.

Two days later, on the 19th of June, the "National Assembly," still only self-styled and possessing only the powers which it had ascribed to itself beyond all forms of law, set to work, nominated its committees, and assumed the sovereignty thus claimed. The Nobles protested (notably the Bishops), and the King, on the advice of Barentin, keeper of the Seals, determined upon immediate resistance. The excuse was taken that the Royal Session, as it was called, in which the King would declare his will, needed the preparation of the hall, and when the

Commons presented themselves at the door of that hall on the next day, the 20th, they found it shut against them. They adjourned to a neighbouring tennis court, and took a solemn corporate oath that they would not separate without giving France a Constitution. They continued to meet, using a church for that purpose, but on the 23rd the Royal Session was opened and the King declared his will.

The reader must especially note that even in this crisis the Crown did not offer a complete resistance. There was an attempt at compromise. Necker would have had a more or less complete surrender, the Queen and her set would have preferred an act of authority which should have annulled all that the Commons had done. What actually happened was a permission by the Crown that the three Orders should meet as one body for certain common interests, but should preserve the system of voting as separate Houses in "all that might regard the ancient and constitutional rights of the three Orders, the Constitution to be given to future Parliaments, feudal property, and the rights and prerogatives of the two senior Houses." As a mere numerical test, such a conclusion would have destroyed the power of the Commons, since, as we have seen, numbers were the weapon of the Commons, who were equal to the two other Houses combined, and if all sat together would, with the Liberal members of the clergy and the nobility, be supreme. But apart from this numerical test, the act of sovereignty affirmed by the National Assembly when it declared itself, and itself only, competent to vote taxes, was annulled. Moreover, the royal declaration ended with a command that on the next day the three Orders should meet separately.

Now at this critical point the King was disobeyed. The current of the time chose the revolutionary bed, and as it began to flow deepened and confirmed its course with every passing day and event. Already the majority of the clergy had joined the National Assembly when it had affirmed its right to sit in spite of the check of the 20th of June. There was a half-hour on that decisive day of the Royal Session, the 23rd of June, when armed force might have been used for the arrest and dispersion of the Deputies. They declared themselves inviolable and their arrest illegal, but there was, of course, no sanction for this decree. As a fact, not a corporal's file was used against them. The next day, the 24th, the majority of the clergy again joined the Commons in their session (in flat defiance of the King's orders), and on the 25th, forty-seven of the nobles followed their example. The King yielded, and on the 27th, two days later, ordered the three Houses to meet together.

The National Assembly was now legally constituted, and set out upon its career. The Crown, the old centre of authority, had abandoned its position, and had confirmed the Revolution, but in doing so it had acted as it were in contradiction with itself. It had made technically legal an illegality which destroyed its own old legal position, but it had done so with ill-will, and it was evident that some counterstroke would be attempted to restore the full powers of the Crown.

At this point the reader must appreciate what forces were face to face in the coming struggle. So far, the illegal and revolutionary act of the 17th of June, the Royal Session which replied to that act upon the 23rd, the King's decree which yielded to the Commons upon the 27th, had all of them been but words. If it came to action, what physical forces were opposed?

On the side of the Crown was the organised armed force which it commanded. For it must never be forgotten that the Crown was the Executive, and remained the Executive right on to the capture of the palace three years later, and the consummation of the Revolution on the 10th of August, 1792. On the side of the National Assembly was without doubt the public opinion of the country (but that is not a force that can be used under arms), and, what was much more to the point, the municipal organisation of France.

Space forbids a full description of the origins and strength of the French municipal system; it is enough to point out that the whole of Gallic civilisation, probably from a moment earlier than Cæsar's invasion, and certainly from the moment when Roman rule was paramount in Gaul, was a *municipal* one. It is so still. The countrysides take their names mainly from their chief towns. The towns were the seats of the bishops, whose hierarchy had preserved whatever could be preserved of the ancient world. In the towns were the colleges, the guilds, the discussion and the corporations which built up the life of the nation. The chief of these towns was Paris. The old systems of municipal government, corrupt and varied as they were, could still give the towns a power of corporate expression. And even where that might be lacking it was certain that some engine would be found for expressing municipal action in a crisis of the sort through which France was now passing. In Paris, for instance, it was seen when the time came for physical force that the College of Electors, who had chosen the representatives for that city, were willing to act at once and spontaneously as a municipal body which should express the initiative of the people. It was the towns, and especially Paris, prompt at spontaneous organisation, ready to arm, and when armed competent to frame a fighting force, which was the physical power behind the Assembly.

What of the physical power behind the King? His power was, as we have said, the Regular Armed forces of the country: the army. But it is characteristic of the moment that only a part of that armed force could be trusted. For an army is never a mere weapon: it consists of living men; and though it will act against the general opinion of its members and will obey orders long after civilians would have broken with the ties of technical and legal authority, yet there is for armies also a breaking point in those ties, and the Crown, I repeat, could not use as a whole the French-speaking and French-born soldiery. Luckily for it, a very great proportion of the French army at that moment consisted of foreign mercenaries.Since the position was virtually one of war, we must consider what was the strategical object of this force. Its object was Paris, the chief of the towns; and round Paris, in the early days of July, the mercenary regiments were gathered from all quarters. That military concentration once effected, the gates of the city held, especially upon the north and upon the west, by encamped regiments and by a particularly large force of cavalry (ever the arm chosen for the repression of civilians), the Crown was ready to act.

On the 11th of July, Necker, who stood for Liberal opinions, was dismissed. A new ministry was formed, and the counter-revolution begun. What followed was the immediate rising of Paris.

The news of Necker's dismissal reached the masses of the capital (only an hour's ride from Versailles) on the afternoon of the 12th, Sunday. Crowds began to gather; an ineffectual cavalry charge in one of the outer open spaces of the city only inflamed the popular enthusiasm, for the soldiers who charged were German mercenary soldiers under the command of a noble. Public forces were at once organised, arms were commandeered from the armourers' shops, the Electoral College, which had chosen the members of the Assembly for Paris, took command at the Guild Hall, but the capital point of the insurrection—what made it possible—was the seizure of a great stock of arms and ammunition, including cannon, in the depot at the Invalides.

With such resources the crowd attacked, at the other end of the city, a fortress and arsenal which had long stood in the popular eye as the symbol of absolute monarchy, the Bastille. With the absurdly insufficient garrison of the Bastille, its apparent impregnability to anything the mob might attempt, the supposed but doubtful treason of its governor in firing upon those whom he had admitted to parley, we are not here concerned. The Bastille was rushed, after very considerable efforts and an appreciable loss in killed and wounded. By the evening of that day, Tuesday, the 14th of July, 1789, Paris had become a formidable instrument of war. The next news was the complete capitulation of the King.

He came on the morrow to the National Assembly, promising to send away the troops; he promised to recall Necker, a municipal organisation was granted to the city, with Bailly for its first mayor, and—a point of capital importance—an armed militia dependent upon that municipality was legally formed, with La Fayette at its head. On the 17th Louis entered Paris to consummate his capitulation, went to the Guild Hall, appeared in the tricoloured cockade, and the popular battle was won.

It behoves us here to consider the military aspect of this definitive act from which the sanction of the Revolution, the physical power behind it, dates.

Paris numbered somewhat under a million souls: perhaps no more than 600,000: the number fluctuated with the season. The foreign mercenary troops who were mainly employed in the repression of the popular feeling therein, were not sufficient to impose anything like a siege. They could at the various gates have stopped the provisioning of the city, but then at any one of those separate points, any one of their detachments upon a long perimeter more than a day's march in circumference would certainly have been attacked and almost as certainly overwhelmed by masses of partially armed civilians.

Could the streets have been cleared while the ferment was rising? It is very doubtful. They were narrow and tortuous in the extreme, the area to be dealt with was enormous, the tradition of barricades not forgotten, and the spontaneous action of that excellent fighting material which a Paris mob contains, had been quite as rapid as anything that could have been effected by military orders.

The one great fault was the neglect to cover the Invalides, but even had the Invalides not been looted, the stock of arms and powder in the city would have been sufficient to have organised a desperate and prolonged resistance. The local auxiliary force (of slight military value, it is true), the "French Guards," as they were called, were wholly with the people. And in general, the Crown must be acquitted of any considerable blunder on the military side of this struggle. It certainly did not fail from lack of will.

The truth is (if we consider merely the military aspect of this military event) that in dealing with large bodies of men who are (a) not previously disarmed, (b) under conditions where they cannot be dispersed, and (c) capable by a national tradition or character of some sort of rapid, spontaneous organisation, the issue will always be doubtful, and the uncertain factor (which is the tenacity, decision and common will of the civilians, to which soldiers are to be opposed) is one that varies within the very widest limits.

In massing the troops originally, the Crown and its advisers estimated that uncertain factor at far too low a point. Even contemporary educated opinion, which was in sympathy with Paris, put it too low. That factor was, as a fact, so high that no armed force of the size and quality which the Crown then disposed of, could achieve its object or hold down the capital.

As for the absurd conception that any body of men in uniform, however small, could always have the better of civilian resistance, however large and well organised, it is not worthy of a moment's consideration by those who interest themselves in the realities of military history. It is worthy only of the academies.

So ends the first phase of the Revolution. It had lasted from the opening of the States-General in May to the middle of July 1789.

II
From the 17th of July 1789 to the 6th of Oct. 1789.

We have seen the military conditions under which the attempt at an armed counter-revolution failed. There follows a short phase of less than three months, whose character can be quickly described.

It was that moment of the Revolution in which ideas had the freest play, in which least had been done to test their application, and most scope remained for pure enthusiasm. That is why we find in the midst of that short phase the spontaneous abandonment of the feudal rights by the nobility. And that is why the violent uprisings all over France continued. It is the period in which the Declaration of the Rights of

Man and of the Citizen, a document which may fittingly stand side by side with the Declaration of Independence (for together they form the noblest monuments of our modern origins), was promulgated. In the same period were the elements of the future Constitution rapidly debated and laid down, and notably that national policy of a *Single Chamber* which the modern French have imprudently abandoned. In that same period, however, appeared, and towards the close of it, another form of resistance on the part of the Crown and of those who advised the Crown. The King hesitated to accept the Declaration of the Rights of Man, and similarly hesitated to promulgate the Decree of the 4th of August in which the nobility had abandoned their feudal dues. It would be foolish to exaggerate the military aspect of what followed. Louis did call in troops, but only in numbers sufficient for personal defence, and we can hardly believe that he intended anything more than to police the surroundings of his throne. But the brigade (for it was no more, nor was it of full strength) which he summoned was sufficient to kindle suspicion; and the determinedly false position of the Queen (who all her life was haunted by the idea that the regular soldiers, especially if they were well dressed and held themselves rigidly, were a sort of talisman) provoked an explosion. A feast was given in which the officers of the Regiment of Flanders, which had just reached Versailles, were entertained by the officers of the Guard. It was made the occasion for a good deal of drunkenness and a violent Royalist manifestation, at which the Queen was present, which she approved, and which some thought she had designed.

The failure of the harvest to relieve the scarcity of bread in Paris, the permanent state of alarm in which Paris had remained, and of suspicion for the safety of the Parliament which it continually entertained since the early part of the summer, needed no more to provoke an outbreak. It is an error to imagine that that outbreak was engineered or that such a movement could have been factitious. Great masses of women (in whom the movement originated), and after them a whole flood of the populace, marched upon Versailles.

There was no direct attack upon the palace, though the palace feared such an attack at any moment. The troops present were sufficient to prevent violence.

La Fayette followed in the night at the head of his new Parisian militia force.

Too much reliance was placed upon the military character of this force; the palace was invaded in the early morning, an attempt to assassinate the Queen on the part of the mob failed, though two of the Guards were killed. And after scenes whose violence and apparent anarchy only masked the common determination of the populace, the royal family were compelled to abandon Versailles and to take up their place in the Tuileries; the Parliament followed them to Paris, and neither King nor Parliament returned again to the suburban palace.

This recapture of the King by Paris is much more significant than a mere impulse of the mob. The King in Paris, the unison of his person with the capital city, had been the very sacrament of French life for century upon century. It was precisely a hundred years since Paris had been abandoned by Louis XIV for Versailles. The significance of that error may be understood by the citizens of an aristocratic country if they will imagine the abandonment of their countrysides by the squires, or, again, the future historian of our modern industrial civilisation may understand it when he describes how the wealthy manufacturers abandoned the cities in which their wealth was made, to dwell outside and apart from the living interests of their people.

With the return of the royal family to Paris, and with the presence of the Assembly within the heart of the national life, one prime factor appears, which is this: that while the National Assembly proceeds step by step to what it imagines to be a complete attainment of democracy (though how partial will soon be seen), the resistance of the Crown is transformed into a resistance of the mere Court. The attack on the Revolution becomes a personal thing. The King is still wholly the chief of the Executive; he can give what commands he wills to the armed force; he controls receipts and payments; he is for all active purposes the Government. But he is no longer considering that prime function of his, nor even using it to restore his old power. He acts henceforward as an individual, and an individual in danger. The Queen, whose view of the Revolution and its dangers had always been a purely personal one, is the directing will in the court-group from this moment, October 1789, onwards; and the chief preoccupation of that group for eighteen months is personal safety. Surrounded by the pomp of the Tuileries and amid all the external appearances of a power still greater than that of any other monarch in Europe, Louis and his wife and their very few immediate and devoted friends and followers thought of the palace as a prison, and never considered their position save as one intolerable.

III

From October 1789 to June 1791.

It is this which must explain all that followed in the succeeding phase, which lasted from these early days of October 1789 to the last week of June 1791. Throughout that period of twenty-one months the King is letting the Revolution take its course, with the fixed idea of thwarting it at last by flying from it, and perhaps conquering it by foreign aid. But even this policy is not consecutively followed. The increasing repugnance of the Court and of the King himself to the revolutionary development forbids a consecutive and purely hypocritical acceptation of the National Assembly's decrees.

Deliberate and calculated intrigue might yet have saved the monarchy and the persons of the royal family. Oddly enough, an ally in the struggle, an excellent intriguer, a saviour of the monarchical institution and a true defender of the royal persons was at hand: it was at hand in the person of Mirabeau.

This man had more and more dominated the Assembly; he had been conspicuous from its first opening days; he had been its very voice in the resistance to the King at Versailles; it was he who had replied to the Master of Ceremonies on June 23, that the Commons would not disperse; it was he who had moved that the persons of the Commons were privileged against arrest. He was of a family noble in station and conspicuous before the people by the wealth and eccentricities of its head, Mirabeau's father. He himself was not unknown even before the Revolution broke out, for his violence, his amours, his intelligence and his debts. He was a few years older than the King and Queen: his personality repelled them; none the less his desire to serve them was sincere; and it was his plan, while retaining the great hold over the National Assembly which his rhetoric and his use of men furnished him, to give to the Court and in particular to the Queen, whom he very greatly and almost reverently admired, such secret advice as might save them. This advice, as we shall see in a moment, tended more and more to be an advice for civil war. But Mirabeau's death at the close of the phase we are now entering (on April 2, 1791), and the increasing fears of the King and Queen, between them prevented any statesmanship at all; they prevented even the statesmanship of intrigue; and the period became, on the side of the Revolution, a rapid and uncontrolled development of its democratic theory (limited by the hesitation of the middle class), and on the side of the Court an increasing demand for mere physical security and flight, coupled with an increasing determination to return, and to restore as a popular monarchy the scheme of the past.

The eighteen months that intervened between the fixing of the Assembly and the royal family in Paris, and the death of Mirabeau, are remarkable for the following points, which must all be considered abreast, as it were, if we are to understand their combined effects.

1. This was the period in which the constructive work of the National Assembly was done, and in which the whole face of the nation was changed. The advising bodies of lawyers called "Parliaments" were abolished (eleven months after the King had come to Paris), the Modern Departments were organised in the place of the old provinces, the old national and provincial militia was destroyed; but (as it is very important to remember) *the old regular army was left untouched.* A new judicature and new rules of procedure were established. A new code sketched out in the place of "Common Law" muddle. In a word, it was the period during which most of those things which we regard as characteristic of the revolutionary work were either brought to their theoretic conclusion or given at least their main lines.

2. Among these constructive acts, but so important that it must be regarded separately, was the Civil Constitution of the Clergy, which will be dealt with at length further in this book; it was the principal work (and the principal error) of that year and a half.

3. The general spirit of the Revolution, more difficult to define than its theory but easy to appreciate as one follows the development of the movement, increased regularly and enormously in intensity during the period. The power of the King, who was still at the head of the Executive, acted more and more as an irritant against public opinion, and—

4. That public opinion began to express itself in a centralised and national fashion, of which the great federation of the 14th of July 1790, in Paris, on the anniversary of the fall of the Bastille, was the nucleus and also the symbol. This federation consisted in delegates from the National Guard throughout the country, and it was of this capital importance: that it introduced into the revolutionary movement a feature of soldiery which made even the regular troops for the most part sympathetic with the enthusiasm of the time.

5. These eighteen months were, again, filled with the movement

of the "Emigration." That movement was, of course, the departure of many of the more prominent of the privileged orders and of a crowd of humbler nobles, as also of a few ecclesiastics, from France. The King's brothers (one fled at the beginning of the emigration, the younger, the Comte d'Artois; the other, the elder, at its close, and coincidently with the flight of the King) must especially be noted in this connection; they formed in company with the more notable of the other emigrants a regular political body, which intrigued continually beyond the frontiers, in Germany and Italy, against the Revolution. And—

6. It was therefore during these months that the ultimate origins of the large European war must be found. The armed body of the emigrants under Condé formed an organised corps upon the Rhine, and though there was not yet the semblance of an armed movement in Europe besides theirs against the French, yet by the *émigrés*, as they were called, were sown the seeds the harvest of which was to be the war of 1792.

I have said that during these months in which most of the constructive work of the Revolution was done, in which the seeds of the great war were sown, and in which the absolute position of the Crown as the head of the Executive was increasingly irritating to the public opinion of the French, and especially of the capital, Mirabeau was the one man who might have preserved the continuity of national institutions by the preservation of the monarchy. He received money from the Court and in return gave it advice. The advice was the advice of genius, but it was listened to less and less in proportion as it was more and more practical. Mirabeau also favoured the abandonment of Paris by the King, but he would have had the King leave Paris openly and with an armed force, withdraw to a neighbouring and loyal centre such as Compiègne, and thence depend upon the fortunes of civil war.

Meanwhile the Queen was determined upon a very different and much more personal plan, into which no conception of statesmanship entered. She was determined to save the persons of her children, herself and her husband. Plans of flight were made, postponed and re-postponed. It was already agreed at the Court that not Mirabeau's plan should be followed, but this plan of mere evasion. The army which Bouillé commanded upon the frontier was to send small detachments along the great road from Paris to the east; the first of these were to meet the royal fugitives a little beyond Chalôns and to escort their carriage eastward; each armed detachment in the chain, as the flight proceeded, was to fall in for its defence, until, once the town of Varennes was reached, the King and Queen should be in touch with the main body of the army.

What was then intended to follow remains obscure. It is fairly certain that the King did not intend to pass the frontier but to take refuge at Montmédy. The conflict that would have inevitably broken out could hardly have been confined to a civil war: foreign armies and the German mercenaries in the French service were presumably to be organised, in case the flight succeeded, for a march upon Paris and the complete restoration of the old state of affairs.

Had Mirabeau lived this rash and unstatesmanlike plan might yet have been avoided; it so happened that he died upon April 2, 1791, and soon after we enter the third phase of the Revolution, which is that leading directly to the great war, and to the fall of the monarchy.

Shortly after Mirabeau's death a tumult, which excessively frightened the royal family, prevented the King and Queen from leaving the palace and passing Easter at St. Cloud, in the suburbs. Though further postponements of their flight followed, the evasion actually took place in the night of the 20th to 21st of June. It very nearly succeeded, but by a series of small accidents, the last of which, the famous ride of Drouet to intercept the fugitives, is among the best-known episodes in history, the King and Queen and their children were discovered and arrested at Varennes, within a few hundred yards of safety, and were brought back to Paris, surrounded by enormous and hostile crowds. With the failure of this attempt at flight in the end of June 1791, ends the third phase of the Revolution.

IV

From June 1791 to September 1792.

To understand the capital effect both of this flight and of its failure, we must once more insist upon the supreme position of the monarchy in the traditions and instinct of French polity. The unwisdom of the flight it would be difficult to exaggerate: it is impossible to exaggerate the moral revolution caused by its failure. It was regarded as virtually an abdication. The strong body of provincial, silent, and moderate opinion, which still centred on the King and regarded it as his function to lead and to govern, was bewildered, and in the main divorced, in the future, from the Crown.

It is an excellent proof of what the monarchy had for so long been to France, that even in such a crisis barely the name of "a republic" was mentioned, and that only in the intellectual circles in Paris. All the constitutional and standing forces of society conspired to preserve the monarchy at the expense of no matter what fictions. The middle class Militia Guard under La Fayette repressed, in what is known as the Massacre of the Champ-de-Mars, the beginnings of a popular movement. The more Radical leaders (among whom was Danton) fled abroad or hid. The Duke of Orleans utterly failed to take advantage of the moment, or to get himself proclaimed regent: the monarchical tradition was too strong.

Immediately after the second anniversary of the taking of the Bastille, in July, the decrees of Parliament created the fiction that the King was not responsible for the flight, that he "had been carried off," and in the following September, though until then suspended from executive power, the King, on taking the oath to the Constitution, was once more at the head of all the forces of the nation.

But all this patching and reparation of the façade of constitutional monarchy (a fiction whose tawdriness is more offensive to the French temper than its falsehood) had come too late. Already the Queen had written to her brother, the Emperor of Austria, suggesting the mobilisation of a considerable force, and its encampment on the frontier, to overawe the revolutionary movement. Her action coincided within a few days with the end of that great Parliament, which had been chosen on the most democratic suffrage, and which had transformed the whole of society and laid the basis of the revolutionary Constitution. With the meeting of the National Assembly's successor on the 1st of October, 1791, war was already possible; that possibility was to be transformed very soon into probability, and at last into actuality.

In the new Parliament the weight, not of numbers but of leadership, fell to a group of enthusiastic and eloquent men who, from the fact that certain of their principal members came from the Gironde, were called *The Girondins*. They represented the purest and the most enthusiastic ideal of democracy, less national, perhaps, than that advocated by men more extreme than they, but of a sort which, from that time to this, has been able to rouse the enthusiasm of historians.

Vergniaud and Isnard were their great orators, Brissot was their intellectual intriguer, and the wife of Roland, one of their members, was, as it were, the soul of the whole group. It was the fact that these men desired war which made war certain, once the temper of this new second Assembly should be felt.

The extremists over against them, to whom I have alluded (known as "the Mountain"), were especially Parisian in character. Robespierre, who had been first an obscure, and later a sectarian orator of the National Assembly, though not sitting in this second Parliament, was perhaps the most prominent figure in that group, for he was the public orator of Paris; and indeed the Mountain was Paris; Paris, whether inside or outside the Parliament; Paris acting as the responsible brain of France. Later, it was the Mountain (that had first opposed the war) which was to ensure the success of the French arms by a rigidity and despotism in action such as the purer and less practical minds of the Girondins abhorred.

On the 3rd of December, 1791 (to quote a fundamental date in the rapid progress towards the war which was to transform the Revolution), the King—writing in a manner which betrays dictation by his wife—begged the King of Prussia (as *she* had begged the Emperor) to mobilise an armed force, and with it to back a Congress that should have for its object the prevention of the spread of the Revolution. That letter was typical of the moment. From both sides tension was rapidly proceeding to the breaking point. Nor was the tension merely upon generalities. The Revolution had broken a European treaty in the annexation of the Papal State of Avignon, and it had broken European conventions when it had abolished in Alsace feudal rights that were possessed by the princes of the empire. It was as though some State to-day, attempting Collectivism, should confiscate, along with other property, securities lying in its banks, but held by the nationals of a foreign State.

On the revolutionary side also there was a definite point at issue, which was the permission accorded within the empire for the emigrants to meet in arms and to threaten the French frontier.

But these precise and legal points were not the true causes of the war. The true causes of the war were the desire of the unreformed European Governments (notably those of Prussia and Austria) that the Revolution should, in their own interests, be checked, and the conviction that their armed forces were easily capable of effecting the destruction of the new French *régime*.

The Court of Vienna refused to accept a just indemnity that was offered the princes of the empire in Alsace for the loss of their old feudal rights; Leopold, the emperor, who was one of the same generation as the French King and Queen, died upon the 1st of March, 1792, and was succeeded by a son only twenty-four years of age and easily persuaded to war.

On the French side, with the exception of the Mountain and notably of Robespierre, there was a curious coalition of opinion demanding war.

The Court and the reactionaries were sufficiently certain of the victory of the Allies to find their salvation in war.

The revolutionary party, that is, the mass of public opinion and the "patriots," as they called themselves, the Girondins, also, and especially, desired war as a sort of crusade for the Revolution; they suffered grievous illusions, as enthusiasts always must, and believed the French armed forces capable of sustaining the shock. The plans had already been drawn up for the campaign (and promptly betrayed to the enemy by the Queen); Dumouriez, an excellent soldier, had from the middle of March 1792 been the chief person in the ministry, and the director of foreign affairs, and a month later, on the 20th of April, war was declared against Austria, or, to be accurate, against "the King of Hungary and Bohemia."

Such was still the official title of Marie Antoinette's nephew, who, though now succeeded to the empire, had not yet been crowned emperor. It was hoped to confine the war to this monarch, and, indeed, the German princes of the empire did not join him (the Landgrave of Hesse-Cassel was an exception). But the one German power that counted most, the kingdom of Prussia, which Dumouriez had especially hoped to keep neutral, joined forces with Austria. The royal letters had done their work.

At this critical moment the French armed forces and the French strongholds were at their worst. The discipline of the army was deplorable. The regular soldiers of the old *régime* had lost from six to nine thousand officers by emigration, and mixed no better than water and oil with the revolutionary volunteers who had been drafted (to the number of over two hundred battalions) into the ranks of the army; moreover, these volunteer battalions were for the most part ill provided, far below their establishment, some only existed on paper; none were trained as soldiers should be trained. In a more orderly time, when the decrees of the Government corresponded with reality, four hundred thousand men would have held the frontier; such a number was in the estimates. As it was, from the Swiss mountains to the English Channel, the French could count on no more than *one-fifth* of that number. Eighty thousand alone were under arms. The full Prussian army was, alone, apart from its allies, close upon treble the size of this disorganised and insufficient force.

Panics at once ludicrous and tragic opened the campaign upon the French side. The King took advantage of them to dismiss his Girondin Ministry and to form a reactionary Government. The Parliament replied by measures useless to the conduct of war, and designed only to exasperate the Crown, which was betraying the nation. It ordered the dismissal of the royal Guard, the formation of a camp of revolutionary Federals outside Paris, the transportation of the orthodox priests; in pursuit of the Court's determination to resist the Assembly and to await the victorious allies, Louis vetoed the last two decrees. La Fayette, who was now in command of the army of the centre, with his headquarters at Sedan, right upon the route of the invasion, declared for the King.

Had the armies of Austria and Prussia moved with rapidity at this moment, the Revolution was at an end. As it was, their mobilisation was slow, and their march, though accurate, leisurely. It gave time for the populace of Paris to demonstrate against the palace and the royal family on the 20th of June. It was not until the first days of August that the main force of the combined monarchs, under the generalship-in-chief of the Duke of Brunswick (who had the reputation of being the best general of his time), set out for the march on Paris. It was not until the 23rd of August that the invaders took the first French frontier town, Longwy.

Meanwhile two very important things had lent to the French, in spite of the wretched insufficiency of their armed force, an intensity of feeling which did something to supply that insufficiency. In the first place, the third anniversary of the Fall of the Bastille, the 14th of July, had called to Paris deputations from all the provinces, many of them armed; this gave the national feeling unity. In the second place, Brunswick had issued from Coblentz, which was his base, upon the 25th of that same month of July, a manifesto which was known in Paris three days later, and which (though certain modern historians have questioned this) undoubtedly set revolutionary opinion ablaze.

This manifesto demanded, in the name of the Allied Army, a complete restoration of the old *régime*, professed to treat the French and their new authorities as rebels subject to military execution, and contained a clause of peculiar gravity, which excited an immediate and exasperated response from Paris. The authorship of this clause lay with Marie Antoinette, and it threatened, if there were any attack upon the palace, to give the capital over to military execution and total subversion.

Two days later the Federals from Marseilles, a middle-class body of excellent citizens, though merely amateurs at soldiering and small in numbers, marched into the city. Their marching song has become famous under the title of the "Marseillaise." They had accomplished the astonishing feat of traversing France, drawing cannon with them, at the rate of eighteen miles a day, in the height of a torrid summer, for close upon a month on end. There is no parallel to such an effort in the history of war, nor did contemporary opinion exaggerate when it saw in the battalion of Marseilles the centre of the coming fight.

The shock between the palace and the populace was joined in the morning of the 10th of August. The palace was held by about six thousand men,* of whom some twelve hundred were regulars of the Swiss Guard. The palace (the Tuileries) was, or should have been, impregnable. The popular attack, we may be certain, would have been beaten back had the connection between the Tuileries and the Louvre on the south been properly cut. The flooring had indeed been removed at this point for some distance, but either the gap was not wide enough or the post was insufficiently guarded; the populace and the Federals, badly beaten in their main attack upon the long front of the palace, succeeded in turning its flank where it joined on to the Louvre; they thus enfiladed the suites of rooms and utterly put an end to the resistance of its garrison.

Meanwhile the King and Queen, the Dauphin and his little sister, with others of the royal household, had taken refuge during the fighting in the hall of the Parliament.

After the victory of the populace their fate was debated and decided upon; they were imprisoned in the Tower of the Temple, a mediæval fortress still standing in the north-east of Paris, and though monarchy was not yet formally abolished, the most extreme spirits which

---

* The reader should be warned that these numbers are hotly disputed. The latest authority will allow no more than 4000. After a full consultation of the evidence I can reduce the garrison to no less than 6000.

the Revolution then contained, and the most vigorous, stepped into the place of the old Executive, with Danton at their head. With them appeared in the seat of Government the spirit of military action, its contempt for forms and its rapid decision. The known accomplices of the supporters of the Court's resistance and alliance with the invaders were arrested by the hundred. The enrolment of volunteers, already enthusiastic throughout France, was supported with the new vigour of official aid; and the Revolution left at once all its old moorings to enter an extreme phase. At the same moment the frontier was crossed and the national soil invaded on the 19th of August.

It is possible that the delay of the Prussians until that moment had been calculated, for the position in France was complicated and their decision to fight had been tardily arrived at. It was the news of the fall of the palace that seems to have decided them. The place, like the date, of this grave event, deserves to be more famous than it is. Brunswick touched what was then French soil, in that little triangle where now German and French Lorraine and Luxembourg meet. The village is called Redange: thence did the privileged of Europe set out to reach Paris and to destroy democracy. The first task occupied them for full twenty-two years, upon the latter they are still engaged.

What forces the French could there bring against Brunswick were contemptuously brushed aside. Four days later he had, as we have seen, taken the frontier stronghold of Longwy; within a week he was in front of Verdun.

Verdun had no chance of resistance, no garrison to call a garrison, and no opportunity for defence. The news that it must fall reached Paris on the morning of a fatal date, the 2nd of September; after its fall there would lie nothing between it and the capital; and from that moment the whole nature of the Revolution is wholly transformed by the psychological effect of war.

V

From the invasion of September 1792 to the establishment
of the Committee of Public Safety, April 1793.

The fifth phase of the French Revolution may be said to date from these first days of September 1792, when the news of the successful invasion was maddening Paris, and when the revolutionary Executive, established upon the ruins of the old dead monarchy and in its image, was firmly in the saddle, up to the establishment of the yet more monarchical "Committee of Public Safety," seven months later. And these seven months may be characterised as follows:—

They were a period during which it was attempted to carry on the revolutionary war against the Governments of Europe upon democratic principles. The attempt failed. In the place of discipline and comprehension and foresight the rising and intense enthusiasm of the moment was depended upon for victory. The pure ideal of the Girondin faction, with the model republic which it hoped to establish, proved wholly insufficient for the conduct of a war; and to save the nation from foreign conquest and the great democratic experiment of the Revolution from disaster, it was necessary that the military and disciplined side of the French, with all the tyranny that accompanies that aspect of their national genius, should undertake the completion of the adventure.

This period opens with what are called the Massacres of September. I have said upon a former page that "the known accomplices and supporters of the Court's alliance with the invaders were arrested by the hundred," upon the fall of the palace and the establishment of a revolutionary Executive with Danton at its head.

These prisoners, massed in the jails of the city, were massacred to the number of eleven hundred by a small but organised band of assassins during the days when the news of the fall of Verdun was expected and reached the capital. Such a crime appalled the public conscience of Europe and of the French people. It must never be confused with the judicial and military acts of the Terror, nor with the reprisals undertaken against rebellion, nor with the gross excesses of mob violence; for though votes in favour of the immediate execution of those who had sided with the enemies of the country were passed in certain primary assemblies, the act itself was the mechanical, deliberate and voluntary choice of a few determined men. It had, therefore, a character of its own, and that character made it stand out for its contemporaries as it should stand out for us: it was murder.

The prisoners were unarmed—nay, though treasonable, they had not actually taken arms; their destruction was inspired, in most of those who ordered it, by mere hatred. Those who ordered it were a small committee acting spontaneously, and Marat was their chief.*

---

* The legend that Danton was connected with the massacres is based on insuf-

It was under the impression of these massacres that the Deputies of the new or third Assembly of the Revolution, known to history as *The Convention*, met in Paris.

This Parliament was to be at first the actual, later the nominal governing power in France during the three critical years that followed; years which were the military salvation of the Revolution, and which therefore permitted the establishment of the democratic experiment in modern Europe.

It was on the 20th of September that the Convention met for its first sitting, which was held in the palace of the Tuileries. During the hours of that day, while it was electing its officials, choosing its Speaker and the rest, the French Army upon the frontier, to its own astonishment and to that of its enemy, managed to hold in check at the cannonade of *Valmy* the allied invaders.

Upon the morrow the new Assembly met in the riding school (the Manège), where the two former Assemblies had also sat. It was about to separate after that day's sitting when one of the members proposed the abolition of Royalty; the Convention voted the reform unanimously and dispersed.

On the third day, the 22nd of September, it was decreed that the public documents should henceforward bear the date "First Year of the Republic"; but there was no solemnity on the occasion; the idea of "No King" was novel and untried; there was as yet no enthusiasm for any save the monarchic form of government. It was not until the title "Republic" began to connote in men's minds political liberty, and had become also the flag, as it were, for the victorious national defence, that the Republican name acquired in our Europe, and from France, that strong and almost religious force which it has since retained.

The check given to the invaders at Valmy (again to the astonishment of both soldiers and statesmen!) determined the campaign. Sickness and the difficulty of communications made the further advance of the invaders impossible. They negotiated for and obtained an unmo-

---

ficient historical foundation. There are several second or third hand stories in support of it, but the chief positive evidence brought forward in this connection is the stamped paper of the Minister of Justice which, it has been amply proved by Dr. Robinet, was taken by a subordinate and without Danton's knowledge or complicity. To the much stupider story that the Federals of Marseilles took part in the massacres, the modern student need pay no attention; it has been destroyed piecemeal and on indefeasible documentary evidence in the monograph of Pollio and Marcel.

lested retreat, and a few weeks later they had re-crossed the frontier.

Meanwhile, in Paris the great quarrel had begun between the Municipal and the National Government, which, because Paris was more decided, more revolutionary, and, above all, more military in temper than the Parliament, was destined to terminate in the victory of the capital. The Girondins still stood in the Assembly for an ideal republic; a republic enjoying to the utmost limit individual liberty in its citizens and the autonomy of local government in every city and parish; but opposed to this ideal, and far more national, was that of the revolutionary extremists, called in the Convention "the Mountain," who had the support of the Municipal Government of Paris (known as "the Commune"), and were capable of French victories in the field. These stood for the old French and soldierly conception of a strong central Government, wherewith to carry on the life-and-death struggle into which the Revolution had now entered: therefore they conquer-

All that autumn the quarrel between France and Europe remained doubtful, for though the armies of the Republic under Dumouriez won the battle of Jemappes, swept across the north-eastern frontier and occupied Belgium, while to the south another French army swept right up to the Rhine, Dumouriez himself knew well enough that a campaign undertaken merely upon enthusiasm, and with troops so mixed in character and many of them so undisciplined, would end fatally. But until the advent of the new year public opinion was not instructed upon these lines, and the revolutionary war seemed to have passed suddenly from the defence of the national territory to a crusade against the kings and the aristocratic Governments of Europe. Enthusiasm, and enthusiasm alone, was the force of the moment. Violent decrees such as the Declaration of Fraternity (which decreed an alliance with all people struggling to be free) and the opening of the Scheldt (a direct violation of treaty rights to which England, among other nations, was a partner) were characteristic of the moment; chief act of all, the King was put upon his trial at the bar of the Parliament.

It was upon the 4th of January, 1793 (the King had already made his will upon Christmas Day), that the chief orator of the Girondins moved that the sentence should be referred to the people for ratification. The fear of civil war more than anything else forbade this just suggestion to pass. Upon the 15th of January the question was put to the Parliament, "whether the King had been guilty of conspiring against public liberty and of attempting the general safety of the State."

Many were absent and many abstained: none replied in the negative; the condemnation of Louis was therefore technically almost a unanimous one.

The voting on these grave issues was what the French call "nominal": that is, each member was called upon "by name" to give his vote—and an expression of opinion as well if he so chose. A second attempt to appeal to the people was rejected by 424 to 283. On the third question, which was the decisive one of the penalty, 721 only could be found to vote, and of these a bare majority of 53 declared for death as against the minority, of whom some voted for the death penalty "conditionally"—that is, not at all—or voted against it. A respite was lost by a majority of 70; and on the 21st of January, 1793, at about ten in the morning, Louis XVI was guillotined.

Then followed war with England, with Holland, and with Spain; and almost at that moment began the inevitable reflux of the military tide. For the French eruption up to the Rhine in the Low Countries and the Palatinate, had no permanent military basis upon which to depend. Dumouriez began to retreat a month after the King's execution, and on the 18th of March suffered a decisive defeat at Neerwinden. It was this retreat, followed by that disaster, which decided the fate of the Girondin attempt to found a republic ideally, individually, and locally free. Already, before the battle of Neerwinden was fought, Danton, no longer a minister, but still the most powerful orator in the Convention, proposed a special court for trying cases of treason—a court which was later called "the Revolutionary Tribunal." The news of Neerwinden prepared the way for a stronger measure and some exceptional form of government; a special Parliamentary committee already formed for the control of ministers was strengthened when, on the 5th of April, after some negotiation and doubt, Dumouriez, despairing of the armies of the Republic, thought to ally his forces with the invaders and to restore order. His soldiers refused to follow him; his treason was apparent; upon the morrow the Convention nominated that first "Committee of Public Safety" which, with its successor of the same name, was henceforward the true despotic and military centre of revolutionary government. It was granted secrecy in deliberation, the virtual though not the theoretic control of the Ministry, sums of money for secret expenditure, and, in a word, all the machinery necessary to a military executive. Rousseau's *Dictator* had appeared, the great mind which had given the *Contrat Social* to be the gospel of the Revolution had also foreseen one of the necessary organs of democracy in its hardest trial; his theory had been proved necessary and true in fact. Nine members formed this first Committee: Barère, who may be called the clerk of it, Danton its genius, and Cambon its financier, were the leading names.

With the establishment of this truly national and traditional thing, whose form alone was novel, but whose power and method were native to all the military tradition of Gaul, the Revolution was saved. We have now chiefly to follow the way in which the Committee governed and in which it directed affairs in the great crisis of the war. This sixth phase lasts for nearly sixteen months, from the beginning of April 1793 to the 28th of July 1794, and it is convenient to divide those sixteen months into two divisions.

VI

From April 1793 to July 1794.

The first division of this period, which ends in the height of the summer of 1793, is the gradual consolidation of the Committee as a new organ of government and the peril of destruction which it runs, in common with the nation it governs at the hands of allied Europe.

The second period includes part of August and all the rest of 1793, and the first seven months of 1794, during which time the Committee is successful in its military effort, the nation is saved, and in a manner curiously dramatic and curiously inconsequential, the martial *régime* of the Terror abruptly ceases.

The first step in the consolidation of the power of the Committee was their letting loose of the Commune of Paris and the populace it governed against the Girondins.

Looked at merely from the point of view of internal politics (upon which most historians have concentrated) the attack of the populace of Paris and their Commune against the Parliament seems to be no more than the end of the long quarrel between the Girondins with their ideal federal republic, and the capital with its instinct for strong centralised government. But in the light of the military situation, of which the Committee of Public Safety were vividly aware, and which it was their business to control, a very different tale may be told.

When the defeats began the Parliament had voted a levy of three hundred thousand men. It was a mere vote which came to very little:

not enough in numbers and still less in moral, for the type of troops recruited under a system of money forfeit and purchased substitutes was wholly beneath the task of the great war.

This law of conscription had been passed upon the 24th of February. The date for its first application was, in many villages, fixed for the 10th of March. All that country which borders the estuary of the Loire, to the north and to the south, a country whose geographical and political peculiarities need not here detain us, but which is still curiously individual, began to resist. The decree was unpopular everywhere, of course, as military service is everywhere unpopular with a settled population. But here it had no ally, for the Revolution and all its works were grossly unpopular as well. The error of the Civil Constitution of the Clergy was a powerful factor in this revolt. The piety and the orthodoxy of this district were and are exceptional. Some such resistance in some such quarter was perhaps expected: what was not expected was its military success.

Four days before the defeat of Neerwinden itself, and four days after the decree of conscription in the villages, a horde of peasantry had taken possession of the town of Chollet in the southern part of this district, Vendée. Three days before the Committee of Public Safety was formed the insurgents had defeated regular forces at Machecoul, and had tortured and put to death their prisoners. The month of April, when the Committee of Public Safety was first finding its seat in the saddle, saw the complete success of the rebels. The forces sent against them were worthless, for all military effort had been concentrated upon the frontier. Most of them were not even what we should call militia. A small force of regulars was to have moved from Orleans, but, before they could attack, Thouars, Parthenay, and Fontenay fell into the power of the rebels. These posts afforded an advanced triangle right into the regularly administered territory of the Republic: the great town of Nantes was outflanked. Even in such a moment the Girondins still clung to their ideal: an individually free and locally autonomous republic. It is little wonder that the temper of Paris refused to support them, or their influence over the Parliament, and we can easily understand how the new Committee supported Paris in its revolt.

That revolt took place on the 31st of May. The forces under the command of the capital did not march, but a deputation of the sections of Paris demanded the arrest of the leading Girondins. The body of the debating hall was invaded by the mob. The Committee of Public Safety pretended to compromise between Paris and the Parliament, but a document, recently analysed, sufficiently proves that their sympathy was with the Parisian attack. They proposed, indeed, to put the armed force of Paris at the disposition of the Assembly: that is, in their own hands.

That day nothing of moment was done, but the Parliament had proved of no strength in the face of the capital. On the frontier the advance of the invaders had begun. The great barrier fortress of Valenciennes relied for its defence upon the neighbouring camp of Famars. The garrison of that camp had been compelled to evacuate it by the advance of the Allied Army upon the 23rd of May, and though some days were to be spent before the heavy artillery of the Austrians could be emplaced, Valenciennes was henceforward at the mercy of its besiegers. There was news that La Vendée was not the only rebellion. Lyons had risen three days before. There had been heavy fighting. The Royalists and the Girondins had combined and had carried the town hall and established an insurrectionary and unelected Municipal Government. Such news, coming immediately after the 31st of May, roused the capital to action. This time the Parisian forces actually marched against the Parliament. The demand for the suspension of the twenty-two named Girondin deputies was made under arms. Much has been written, and by the best historians, to make of this successful day a mere conquest by the Commune of Paris over the Parliament. Though Barère and Danton both protested in public, it was in reality their politics that conquered with Paris. To the twenty-two names that the forces of Paris had listed, seven were added. The great Girondins, Brissot, Vergniaud and the rest, were not indeed imprisoned, they were considered "under arrest in their houses." But the moral authority of the Convention as an administrative machine, not as a legislative one, was broken on this day, the 2nd of June, 1793. Paris had ostensibly conquered, but the master who was stronger than ever and whom Paris had served, was the Committee of Public Safety.

This first Committee of Public Safety endured to the 10th of July. In the midst of such a war and of such an internal struggle the Convention had voted (upon the initiative of the Committee of Public Safety) the famous Constitution of '93, that prime document of democracy which, as though to mock its own ideal, has remained no more than a written thing from then until now. Therein will be found universal suffrage, therein the yearly Parliament, therein the referendum, therein the elected Executive—a thing no Parliament would ever give us to-day. The Constitution was passed but three weeks after the successful insurrection of Paris. A fortnight later still, on the 10th of July, the first of the Committees of Public Safety was followed by its successor.

All this while the Vendeans were advancing. Nantes, indeed, had held out against the rebels, but as we shall see in a moment, the Republican troops had not yet made themselves good. The rebellion of Lyons was fortifying itself, and a week later was to execute the Radical Chalier. Marseilles was rising. On the 10th of July the Convention summoned to its bar Westermann, the friend of Danton, who had just suffered defeat at the hands of the western rebels.

It is well to note at this point one of those small individual factors which determine the fate of States. Danton, the master of all that first movement towards centralisation, the man who had made the 10th of August, who had negotiated with the Prussians after Valmy, who had determined upon and formed a central government against the Girondin anarchy—had broken down. His health was gone. He was a giant in body, but for the moment he had tired himself out.

The renewing of his Committee was proposed: he was thrust out from the new choice. Barère remained to link the old Committee with the new. A violent sectarian Calvinist pastor, Jeanbon Saint-André, among the bravest and most warped of the Revolutionaries; Couthon, a friend of Robespierre; Saint-Just, a still more intimate friend (a young, handsome, enormously courageous and decisive man), entered, with others to the number of nine, the new Committee. Seventeen days later, on the 27th of July, Robespierre replaced one of the minor members thus chosen. He had precisely a year to live, and it is the moment for fixing before the reader's mind the nature of his career.

Robespierre was at this moment the chief figure in the eyes of the crowd, and was soon to be the chief revolutionary figure in the eyes of Europe: that is the first point. The second is of equal importance, and is far less generally recognised. He was not, and was never destined to be, the chief force in the revolutionary Government.

As to the first point, Robespierre had attained this position from the following combination of circumstances: first, alone of the revolutionary personalities, he had been continually before the public eye from the beginning; he had been a member of the first Parliament of all and had spoken in that Parliament in the first month of its sessions.

Though then obscure in Versailles, he was already well known in his province and native town of Arras.

Secondly, this position of his in the public eye was maintained without a break, and his position and reputation had increased by accumulation month after month for the whole four years. No one else was left in the political arena of whom this could be said. All the old reactionaries had gone, all the moderate men had gone; the figures of 1793 were all new figures—except Robespierre; and he owed this continued and steady increase of fame to:—

Thirdly, his conspicuous and vivid sincerity. He was more wholly possessed of the democratic faith of the *Contrat Social* than any other man of his time: he had never swerved from an article of it. There is no better engine for enduring fame than the expression of real convictions. Moreover—

Fourthly, his speeches exactly echoed the opinions of his audience, and echoed them with a lucidity which his audience could not have commanded. Whether he possessed true eloquence or no is a matter still debated by those who are scholars in French letters. But it is certain that he had in his own time all the effects of a great orator, though his manner was precise and cold.

Fifthly, he was possessed of a consistent body of doctrine: that is, he was not only convinced of the general democratic creed which his contemporaries held, and he not only held it unswervingly and uncorruptedly, but he could supplement it with a system of morals and even something which was the adumbration of religion.

Sixthly, he had, as such characters always can, but not often do, gather round themselves, a group of intensely devoted personal admirers and supporters, chief of whom was the young and splendidly courageous Saint-Just.

It was the combination of all these things, I say, which made Robespierre the chief personality in the public eye when he entered the Committee of Public Safety on the 27th of July, 1793.

Now let it be noted that, unlike his follower Saint-Just, and exceedingly unlike Danton, Robespierre possessed none of those military qualities without which it is impossible to be responsible for government over a military nation—especially if that nation be in the act of war: and such a war! The Committee of Public Safety was the Cæsar of revolutionary France. Robespierre as a member of that Cæsar was hopeless. His popularity was an advantage to his colleagues in the Committee, but his conception of action upon the frontiers was vague, personal, and futile. His ambition for leadership, if it existed, was subordinate to his ambition to be the saviour of his people and of their democratic experiment, and he had no comprehension of those functions of leadership by which it can co-ordinate detail and impose a plan of action. Robespierre, therefore, in every crisis of the last year we are about to study, yielded to his colleagues, never impressed them and never led them, and yet (it was the irony of his fate) was imagined by his fellow countrymen and by the warring Governments of Europe to be the master of them all.

The first weeks after his appearance in the Committee of Public Safety were the critical weeks of the whole revolutionary movement. The despotic action of Paris (which I have concluded to be secretly supported by the Committee)* had provoked insurrection upon all sides in the provinces. Normandy had protested, and on the 13th of July a Norman girl stabbed Marat to death. Lyons, as we have seen, had been some weeks in revolt; Marseilles had rebelled in the first week of June, Bordeaux and the whole department of the Gironde had of course risen, for their men were at stake. Later Toulon, the great naval depot of France, revolted: a reactionary municipal provincial Government was formed in that port, the little boy imprisoned in the Temple, heir to the kingdom, was proclaimed under the title of Louis XVII, and before the end of August the English and Spanish fleets had been admitted into the harbour and an excellent foreign garrison was defending the town against the national Government.

Meanwhile the Allies upon the Belgian frontier were doing what they could, taking fortress after fortress, and while Mayence was falling on the Rhine, Valenciennes and Condé were capitulating on the north-eastern border, and a portion of the Allied Army was marching to besiege Dunquerque. The insurrection in Vendée, which had broken out in the early part of the year, though checked by the resistance of Nantes, was still successful in the field.

It was in the month of August that a successful effort was made. Carnot, who soon proved the military genius of the Revolution,

---

* On p. 403 of my monograph on Danton (Nisbet & Co., 1899) the reader will find an unpublished report of the Committee of Public Safety, drawn up immediately before the destruction of the Girondins on the 31st of May. It forms, in my view, conclusive evidence, read in the light of their other actions, of the Committee's determination to side with Paris.

entered the Committee of Public Safety. On the 23rd of the month a true levy, very different from the futile and insufficiently applied attempt of the spring, was forced upon the nation by a vote in Parliament. It was a levy of men, vehicles, animals and provision, and soon furnished something not far short of half a million soldiers. With September the tide turned, the first victory in this crisis of the struggle, Hoondschoote, relieved Dunquerque in the early days of September. By mid-October a second and decisive victory, that of Wattignies, relieved Maubeuge. Lyons had been taken, Normandy was pacified long before; by the end of the year Toulon was reoccupied, and at the same time the last cohesive force of the Vendeans destroyed.

But meanwhile the crisis had had a double effect, moral and material. The moral effect had been a sort of national madness in which the most extreme measures were proposed and many of them carried through with what one may call a creative audacity. The calendar itself was changed, the week itself abolished, the months re-named and re-adjusted. Such an act sufficiently symbolises the mental attitude of the Revolutionaries. They were determined upon a new earth.

There went with this the last and most violent attack upon what was believed to be the last remnants of Catholicism in the country, a hideous persecution of the priesthood, in which an uncounted number of priests died under the rigours of transportation or of violence. The reprisals against the rebels varied from severity of the most awful kind to cruelty that was clearly insane, and of which the worst examples took place at Arras and at NantesIn all this turmoil the governing centre of the country, the Committee of Public Safety, not only kept its head but used the enormous forces of the storm for the purposes of achieving military success, under that system known as "the Terror," which was for them no more than martial law, and an engine of their despotic control. Of the two thousand and more that passed before the revolutionary tribunal and were executed in Paris, the large majority were those whom the Committee of Public Safety judged to be obstacles to their military policy; and most were men or women who had broken some specific part of the martial code which the Government had laid down. Some were generals who had failed or were suspected of treason; and some, among the most conspicuous, were politicians who had attempted to check so absolute a method of conducting the war.

Of these the greatest was Danton. Before the end of 1793 he began to protest against the system of the Terror; he believed, perhaps, that the country was now safe in the military sense and needed such rigours no more. But the Committee disagreed, and were evidence available we should perceive that Carnot in particular determined that such opposition must cease. Danton and his colleagues—including Desmoulins, the journalist of the Revolution and the chief publicist who promoted the days of July 1789—were executed in the first week of April 1794.

Parallel to this action on the part of the Committee was their sudden attack upon men of the other extreme: the men whose violence, excessive even for that time, threatened to provoke reaction. Hébert was the chief of these, the spokesman of the Commune of Paris; and he also perished.

Meanwhile the Committee had permitted other persecutions and other deaths, notably that of the Queen. A sane policy would have demanded that she should be kept a hostage: she was sacrificed to the desire for vengeance, and her head fell on the same day on which the decisive battle of Wattignies was won. Later the King's sister, Madame Elisabeth, was sacrificed to the same passions, and with her must be counted a certain proportion of the victims whose destruction could be no part of the Committee's scheme, and proceeded purely from the motives of an ancient hatred, though in the case of many of these who were of aristocratic birth or of influence through their wealth, it is not easy to determine how far the possibility of their intrigue with the foreigner may not have led them to the scaffold.

In the last four months of the period we are considering in this book, through April, that is, after the execution of Danton, through May and June and almost to the end of July, Robespierre appears with a particular prominence. Fads or doctrines of his own are admitted upon the Statute Book of the Revolution, notably his religious dogmas of a personal God and of the immortality of the soul. Nay, a public solemnity is arranged in honour of such matters, and he is the high priest therein. The intensity of the idolatry he received was never greater; the numbers that shared it were, perhaps, diminishing. It is certain that he did not appreciate how far the supports of his great popularity were failing. It is certain that he saw only the increasing enthusiasm of his immediate followers. The Committee still used him as their tool—notably for an increase of the Terror in June, but it is possible that for the first time in all these months he began to attempt some sort of authority within the Committee: we know, for instance, that he quarrelled with Carnot, who was easily the strongest man therein.

In the past they had permitted him to indulge a private policy where it did not interfere with the general military plan. He was largely responsible, not through his own judgment but from his desire to voice opinion, for the trial and execution of the Queen. He had temporised when Danton was beginning his campaign against the Terror at the end of 1793, and it is an ineffaceable blot upon his memory and his justly earned reputation for integrity and sincerity, that he first permitted and then helped towards Danton's execution. We may presume from the few indications we have that he protested against it in the secret counsels of the Committee, but he had yielded, and what is more, since Saint-Just desired to be Danton's accuser he had furnished Saint-Just with notes against Danton. Though it was the Committee who were morally responsible for the extreme extension of the Terror which proceeded during those last few months, Robespierre had the unwisdom to act as their instrument, to draft their last decrees, and, believing the Terror to be popular, to support it in public. It was this that ruined him. The extreme Terrorists, those who were not yet satiated with vengeance, and who hated and feared a popular idol, determined to overthrow him.

The mass of those who might be the next victims and who, knowing nothing of the secret councils of the Committee, imagined Robespierre to be what he posed as being, the master of the Committee, were eager for his removal. In his fictitious character as the supposed chief power in the State, all the growing nausea against the Terror was directed against his person.

Coincidently with such forces, the Committee, whom, relying upon his public position, he had begun to interfere with, and probably to check in their military action (he certainly had attempted unsuccessfully to save certain lives against the decision of his colleagues), determined to be rid of him. The crisis came in the fourth week of July: or as the revolutionary calendar then went, in the second week of Thermidor. He was howled down in the Parliament, an active and clever conspiracy had organised all the latent forces of opposition to him; he still so trusted in his popularity that the scene bewildered him, and he was still so beloved and so ardently followed, that when at that same sitting he was outlawed, his brother sacrificed himself to follow him. Saint-Just was included in the sentence, and his strict friend Lebas voluntarily accepted the same doom.

What followed was at first a confusion of authority; put under arrest, the governor of the prison to which Robespierre was dispatched refused to receive him. He and his sympathisers met in the Hôtel de Ville after the fall of darkness, and an attempt was made to provoke an insurrection. There are many and confused accounts of what immediately followed at midnight, but two things are certain: the populace refused to rise for Robespierre, and the Parliament, with the Committee at its back, organised an armed force which easily had the better of the incipient rebellion at the Hôtel de Ville. It is probable that Robespierre's signature was needed to the proclamation of insurrection: it is certain that he did not complete it, and presumable that he would not act against all his own theories of popular sovereignty and the general will. As he sat there with the paper before him and his signature still unfinished, the armed force of the Parliament burst into the room, a lad of the name of Merda aimed a pistol from the door at Robespierre, and shot him in the jaw. (The evidence in favour of this version is conclusive.) Of his companions, some fled and were captured, some killed themselves, most were arrested. The next day, the 10th Thermidor, or 28th of July, 1794, at half-past seven in the evening, Robespierre, with twenty-one others, was guillotined.

The irony of history would have it that the fall of this man, which was chiefly due to his interference with the system of the Terror, broke all the moral force upon which the Terror itself had resided; for men had imagined that the Terror was his work, and that, he gone, no excuse was left for it. A reaction began which makes of this date the true term in that ascending series of revolutionary effort which had by then discussed every aspect of democracy, succeeded in the military defence of that experiment, and laid down, though so far in words only, the basis of the modern State.

CHAPTER V

THE MILITARY ASPECT OF THE REVOLUTION

The Revolution would never have achieved its object: on the contrary, it would have led to no less than a violent reaction against those principles which were maturing before it broke out, and which it carried to triumph, had not the armies of revolutionary France proved successful in the field; but the grasping of this mere historic fact, I mean the success of the revolutionary armies, is unfortunately no simple matter.

We all know that as a matter of fact the Revolution was, upon the whole, successful in imposing its view upon Europe. We all know that from that success as from a germ has proceeded, and is still proceeding, modern society. But the nature, the cause and the extent of the military success which alone made this possible, is widely ignored and still more widely misunderstood. No other signal military effort which achieved its object has in history ended in military disaster—yet this was the case with the revolutionary wars. After twenty years of advance, during which the ideas of the Revolution were sown throughout Western civilisation, and had time to take root, the armies of the Revolution stumbled into the vast trap or blunder of the Russian campaign; this was succeeded by the decisive defeat of the democratic armies at Leipsic, and the superb strategy of the campaign of 1814, the brilliant rally of what is called the Hundred Days, only served to emphasise the completeness of the apparent failure. For that masterly campaign was followed by Napoleon's first abdication, that brilliant rally ended in Waterloo and the ruin of the French army. When we consider the spread of Grecian culture over the East by the parallel military triumph of Alexander, or the conquest of Gaul by the Roman armies under Cæsar, we are met by political phenomena and a political success no more striking than the success of the Revolution. The

Revolution did as much by the sword as ever did Alexander or Cæsar, and as surely compelled one of the great transformations of Europe. But the fact that the great story can be read to a conclusion of defeat disturbs the mind of the student.

Again, that element fatal to all accurate study of military history, the imputation of civilian virtues and motives, enters the mind of the reader with fatal facility when he studies the revolutionary wars.

He is tempted to ascribe to the enthusiasm of the troops, nay, to the political movement itself, a sort of miraculous power. He is apt to use with regard to the revolutionary victories the word "inevitable," which, if ever it applies to the reasoned, willing and conscious action of men, certainly applies least of all to men when they act as soldiers.

There are three points which we must carefully bear in mind when we consider the military history of the Revolution.

First, that it succeeded: the Revolution, regarded as the political motive of its armies, won.

Secondly, that it succeeded through those military aptitudes and conditions which happened to accompany, but by no means necessarily accompanied, the strong convictions and the civic enthusiasm of the time.

Thirdly, that the element of chance, which every wise and prudent reasoner will very largely admit into all military affairs, worked in favour of the Revolution in the critical moments of the early wars.

With these points fixed, and with a readiness to return to them when we have appreciated the military story, it is well to begin our study by telling that story briefly, and upon its most general lines. In so doing, it will be necessary to cover here and there points which have already been dealt with in this book, but that is inevitable where one is writing of the military aspect of any movement, for it is impossible to deal with that aspect save as a living part of the whole: so knit into national life is the business of war.

ONE

When the Revolution first approached action, the prospect of a war between France and any other great Power of the time—England, Prussia, the Empire, or let us say Russia, or even Spain—was such a prospect as might have been entertained at any time during the past two or three generations of men.

For pretty well a hundred years men had been accustomed to the consideration of dynastic quarrels supported by a certain type of army, which in a moment I shall describe.

I have called these quarrels dynastic; that is, they were mainly quarrels between the ruling houses of Europe: were mainly motived by the desire of each ruling house to acquire greater territory and revenue, and were limited by the determination of all the ruling houses to maintain certain ideas inviolate, as, for instance, the sacredness of monarchy, the independence of individual States, etc. Though they were in the main dynastic, yet in proportion as a dynasty might represent a united nation, they were national also. The English oligarchy was in this respect peculiar and more national than any European Government of its time. It is also true to say that the Russian despotism had behind it, in most of its military adventures and in all its spirit of expansion, the subconscious agreement of the people.

Still, however national, the wars of the time preceding the Revolution moved within a fixed framework of ideas, as it were, which no commander and no diplomatist dreamed of exceeding. A, the crowned head of a State, would have some claims against B, the crowned head of another State, with regard to certain territories. C, the crowned head or Government of a third State, would remain neutral or ally himself with either of the two; if he allied himself, then, as a rule, it was with the weaker against the stronger, in order to guarantee himself against too great an increase on the part of a rival. Or, again, a rebellion would break out against the power of A in some part of his dominions; then would B, somewhat reluctantly (as the almost unlimited right of an existing executive was still a strong dogma in men's minds), tend to ally himself with the rebels in order to diminish the power of A.

Human affairs have always in them very strongly and permanently inherent, the character of a sport: the interest (at any rate of males) in the conduct of human life is always largely an interest of seeing that certain rules are kept, and certain points won, according to those rules. We must, therefore, beware of ridiculing the warfare of the century preceding the Revolution under the epithet of "a game." But it is true of that warfare, and honourably true, that it attempted limited things in a limited manner; it did not attempt any fundamental change in society; it was not overtly—since the Thirty Years' War at least—a struggle of ideas; it was conducted on behalf of known and limited interests for known and highly limited objects, and the instruments with which it was conducted were instruments artificial and segregated from the general life of nations.

These instruments were what have been called the "professional" armies. The term is very insufficient, and, in part, misleading. The gentry of the various Powers, mixed with whom were certain adventurers not always of gentle blood, were the officers that led these forces; and for the major part of the gentry in most European countries, the military career was the chief field of activity. The men whom they led were not a peasantry nor a working class, still less a civic force in which the middle class would find itself engaged: they were the poorest and the least settled, some would have said the dregs of European life. With the exception here and there of a man—usually a very young man whom the fabled romance of this hard but glorious trade had attracted—and with the exception of certain bodies that followed in a mass and by order the relics of a feudal lordship, the armies of the period immediately preceding the Revolution were armies of very poor men, who had sold themselves into a sort of servitude often exciting and even adventurous, but not, when we examine it minutely, a career that a free man would choose. The men were caught by economic necessity, by fraud, and in other ways, and once caught were held. No better proof of this could be found than the barbarous severity of the punishments attached to desertion, or to minor forms of indiscipline. So held, they were used for the purposes of the game, not only in what would make them serviceable instruments of war, but also in what would make them pleasing to their masters. Strict alignment, certain frills of parade and appearance, all that is required in a theatre or in a pretentious household, appear in the military regulations of the time.

I must not in all this be supposed to be belittling that great period between 1660 and 1789, during which the art of war was most thoroughly thought out, the traditions of most of our great European armies fixed, and the permanent military qualities which we still inherit developed. The men so caught as private soldiers could not but enjoy the game when it was actively played, for men of European stock will always enjoy the game of war; they took glory in its recital and in its memories; to be a soldier, even under the servile conditions of the time, was a proper subject for pride, and it is further to be remarked that the excesses of cruelty discoverable in the establishment of their discipline were also accompanied by very high and lasting examples of military virtue. The behaviour of the English contingents at Fontenoy afford but one of many examples of what I mean.

Still, to understand the wars of the Revolution we must clearly establish the contrast between the so-called professional armies which preceded that movement and the armies which the Revolution invented, used, and bequeathed to the modern world.

So also, to revert to what was said above, we must recall the dynastic and limited character of the wars in which the eighteenth century had been engaged; at the outbreak of the Revolution no other wars were contemplated by men.

Had you spoken, for instance, at any moment in 1789, to a statesman, whether of old experience or only introduced to political life by the new movement, of the position of Great Britain, he would at once have discussed that position in the terms of Great Britain's recent defeat at the hands of France in the affair of the American colonies. Had you discussed with him the position of Prussia he would at once have argued it in connection with Prussia's secular opposition to Austria and the Empire. Had you asked him how he considered Spain, he would have spoken of the situation of Spain as against France in the light of the fact that Spain was a Bourbon monarchy allied in blood to the French throne. And so forth. No true statesman imagined at the time, nor, indeed, for many years, that a war of *ideas*, nor even, strictly speaking, of *nations*, was possible. Even when such a war was actually in process of waging, the diplomacy which attempted to establish a peace, the intrigues whereby alliances were sought, or neutrality negotiated, were dependent upon the older conception of things; and the historian is afforded, as he regards this gigantic struggle, the ironic satisfaction of seeing men fighting upon doctrines the most universal conceivable and yet perpetually changing their conduct during the struggle according to conceptions wholly particular, local and ephemeral, and soon to be entirely swept away by time.

Napoleon himself must needs marry an Austrian archduchess as part of this old prejudice, and for years brains as excellent as Danton's or Talleyrand's conjecture the possibility of treating now England, now Prussia, as neutral to the vast attempt of the French to destroy privilege in European society!

One may say that for two years the connection of the revolutionary movement with arms had no aspect save that of civil war. True, whenever a considerable change is in progress in society the possibility of foreign war in connection with it must always arise. Were some European State, for instance, to make an experiment in Collectivism to-day, the chance of foreign intervention would certainly be discussed by the promoters of that experiment. But no serious danger of an armed struggle between the French and any of their neighbours in connection with the political experiment of the Revolution was imagined by the mass of educated men in France itself nor without the boundaries of France during those first two years. And, I repeat, the military aspect of those years was confined to civil tumult. Nevertheless, that aspect is not to be neglected. The way in which the French organised their civil war (and there was always something of it present from the summer of 1789 onwards) profoundly affected the foreign war that was to follow: for in their internal struggles great masses of Frenchmen became habituated to the physical presence, millions to the discussion, of arms.

It is, as we have seen in another part of this book, a repeated and conspicuous error to imagine that the first revolutionary outbreaks were not met sufficiently sternly by royal troops. On the contrary, the royal troops were used to the utmost and were defeated. The populace of the large towns, and especially of Paris, proved itself capable of military organisation and of military action. When to this capacity had been added the institution of the militia called the National Guard, there were already the makings of a nation wholly military.Much in this exceptional and new position must be ascribed to the Gallic character. It may be said that from the fall of the Roman Empire to the present day that character has been permanently and of its own volition steeped in the experience of organised fighting. Civil tumult has been native to it, the risk of death in defence of political objects has been equally familiar, and the whole trade of arms, its necessary organisation, its fatigues and its limiting conditions, have been very familiar to the population throughout all these centuries. But beyond this the fact that the Revolution prepared men in the school of civil tumult was of the first advantage for its later aptitude against foreign Powers.

It is always well in history to fix a definite starting-point for any political development, and the starting-point of the revolutionary wars may easily be fixed at the moment when Louis, his queen and the royal children attempted to escape to the frontier and to the Army of the Centre under the command of Bouillé. This happened, as we have seen, in June 1791.

Many factors combine to make that date the starting-point. In the first place, until that moment no actual proof had been apparent in the eyes of European monarchs of the captivity of their chief exemplar, the king of France.

The wild march upon Versailles, in the days of October 1789, had its parallel in a hundred popular tumults with which Europe was familiar enough for centuries. But the rapidly succeeding reforms of the year 1790, and even the great religious blunder of 1791, had received the signature and the public assent of the Crown. The Court, though no longer at Versailles, was splendid, the power of the King over the Executive still far greater than that of any other organ in the State, and indefinitely greater than that of any other individual in the State. The talk of captivity, of insult and the rest, the outcries of the emigrants and the perpetual complaint of the French royal family in its private relations, seemed exaggerated, or at any rate nothing to act upon, until there came the shock of the King's attempted flight and recapture. This clinched things; and it clinched them all the more because more than one Court, and especially that of Austria, believed for some days that the escape had been successful.

Again, the flight and its failure put the army into a ridiculous posture. Action against the Revolution was never likely, so long as the discipline and steadiness of the French army were believed in abroad. But the chief command had hopelessly failed upon that occasion, and it was evident that the French-speaking troops could not easily be trusted by the Executive Government or by their own commanders. Furthermore, the failure of the flight leads the Queen, with her vivacity of spirit and her rapid though ill-formed plans, to turn for the first time to the idea of military intervention. Her letters suggesting this (in the form of a threat rather than a war, it is true) do not begin until after her capture at Varennes.

Finally, coincident with that disaster was the open mention of a Republic, the open suggestion that the King should be deposed, and the first definite and public challenge to the principles of monarchy which the Revolution had thrown down before Europe.

We are, therefore, not surprised to find that this origin of the military movement was followed in two months by the Declaration of Pillnitz.

With the political nature of that Declaration one must deal elsewhere. Its military character must here be observed.

The Declaration of Pillnitz corresponded as nearly as possible to what in the present day would be an order preparatory to mobilising a certain proportion of the reserve. It cannot with justice be called equivalent to an order *calling out* all the reserves, still less equivalent to an order mobilising upon a war footing the forces of a modern nation, for such an action is tantamount to a declaration of war (as, for instance, was the action of the English Government before the South African struggle), and Pillnitz was very far from that. But Pill-nitz was certainly as drastic a military proceeding as would be the public intimation by a group of Powers that the reserves had been warned in connection with their quarrel against another Power. It was, for instance, quite as drastic as the action of Austria against Servia in 1908. And it was intended to be followed by such submission as is expected to follow upon the threat of superior force.

Such was the whole burden of Marie Antoinette's letters to her brother (who had called the meeting at Pillnitz), and such was the sense in which the politicians of the Revolution understood it.

All that autumn and winter the matter chiefly watched by foreign diplomatists and the clearest of French thinkers was the condition of the French forces and of their command. Narbonne's appointment to the War Office counted more than any political move, Dumouriez' succession to him was the event of the time. Plans of campaign were drawn up (and promptly betrayed by Marie Antoinette to the enemy), manifold occasions for actual hostilities were discovered, the Revolu-tion challenged the Emperor in the matter of the Alsatian princes, the Emperor challenged, through Kaunitz, the Revolution in a letter directly interfering with the internal affairs of France, and pretending to a right of *ingérence* therein; and on the 20th of April, 1792, war was declared against the Empire. Prussia thereupon informed the French Government that she made common cause with the Emperor, and the revolutionary struggle had begun.

The war discovered no serious features during its first four months: so slow was the gathering and march of the Allies; but the panics into which the revolutionary troops fell in the first skirmishes, their lack of discipline, and the apparent breakdown of the French military power, made the success of the Invasion in Force, when it should come, seem certain. The invading army did not cross the frontier until more than a week after the fall of the palace. Longwy capitulated at once; a week later, in the last days of August, the great frontier fortress of Verdun was summoned. It capitulated almost immediately.

TWO

On the 2nd of September Verdun was entered by the Prussians, and a little outside the gates of the town, near a village bearing the name of Regret, the allied camp was fixed. Rather more than a week later, on the 11th, the Allies marched against the line of the Argonne.

The reader will remember that this moment, with the loss of the frontier fortresses Longwy and Verdun, and the evidence of demoralisation which that afforded, was also the moment of the September massacres and of the horrors in Paris. Dumouriez and the mixed French force which he commanded had been ordered by the Ministers of War to hold the line of the Argonne against which the Allies were marching. And here it is well to explain what was meant in a military sense by this word "line."

The Argonne is a long, nearly straight range of hills running from the south northward, a good deal to the west of north.

Their soil is clay, and though the height of the hills is only three hundred feet above the plain, their escarpment or steep side is towards the east, whence an invasion may be expected. They are densely wooded, from five to eight miles broad, the supply of water in them is bad, in many parts undrinkable; habitation with its provision for armies and roads extremely rare. It is necessary to insist upon all these details because the greater part of civilian readers find it difficult to understand how formidable an obstacle so comparatively unimportant a feature in the landscape may be to an army upon the march. It was quite impossible for the guns, the wagons, and therefore the food and the ammunition of the invading army, to pass through the forest over the drenched clay land of that wet autumn save where proper roads existed. These were only to be found wherever a sort of natural pass negotiated the range.

Three of these passes alone existed, and to this day there is very little choice in the crossing of these hills. The accompanying sketch will explain their disposition. Through the southernmost went the great high road from the frontier and Verdun to Paris. At the middle one (which is called the Gap of Grandpré) Dumouriez was waiting with his incongruous army. The third and northern one was also held, but less strongly. The obvious march for an unimpeded invader would have been from Verdun along the high road, through the southern pass at "Les Islettes," and so to Châlons and on to Paris. But Dumouriez, marching down rapidly from the north, had set an advanced guard to hold that pass and was lying himself with the mass of the army on the pass to the north of it at Grandpré. Against Grandpré the Prussians marched, and meanwhile the Austrians were attacking

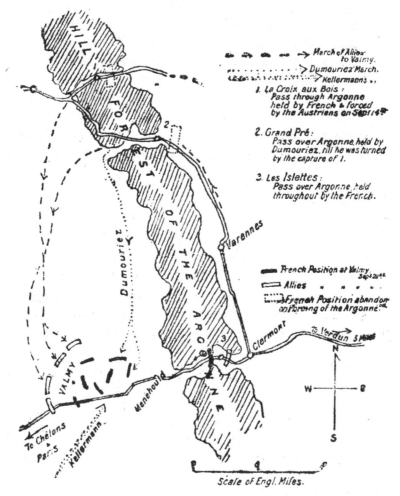

March of Allies to Valmy.
Dumouriez March.
Kellermann's

1. La Croix aux Bois :
Pass through Argonne held by French & forced by the Austrians on Sept 14ᵗ

2. Grand Pré :
Pass over Argonne, held by Dumouriez, till he was turned by the capture of 1.

3. Les Islettes :
Pass over Argonne, held throughout by the French.

French Position at Valmy, Sep 20ᵗ
Allies
French Position abandoned on forcing of the Argonne.

Scale of Engl. Miles.

Sketch Map, showing the turning of the positions on the Argonne and the Cannonade at Valmy, September 1792.

the further pass to the north. Both were forced. Dumouriez fell back southward to St. Menehould. Meanwhile Kellermann was coming up from Metz to join him, and all the while the main pass at "Les Islettes," through which the great road to Paris went, continued to be held by the French.

The Prussians and the Austrians joined forces in the plain known as the Champagne Pouilleuse, which lies westward of Argonne. It will be seen that as they marched south along this plain to meet Dumouriez and to defeat him, their position was a peculiar one: they were nearer the enemy's capital than the enemy's army was, and yet they had to fight with their backs to that capital, and their enemy the French had to fight with their faces towards it. Moreover, it must be remarked that the communications of the Allied Army were now of a twisted, round-about sort, which made the conveyance of provisions and ammunition slow and difficult—but they counted upon an immediate destruction of Dumouriez' force and after that a rapid march on the capital.

On September 19 Kellermann came up from the south and joined hands with Dumouriez near St. Menehould, and on the morning of the 20th his force occupied a roll of land on which there was a wind-mill and immediately behind which was the village of Valmy; from this village the ensuing action was to take its name. It must here be insisted upon that both armies had been subjected to the very worst weather for more than a fortnight, but of the two the Prussian force had suffered from this accident much more severely than the French. Dysentery had already broken out, and the length and tortuousness of their communications were greatly emphasised by the condition of the roads.

On the morning of that day, the 20th of September, a mist impeded all decisive movements. There was an encounter, half accidental, between an advanced French battery and the enemy's guns, but it was not until mid-morning that the weather lifted enough to show each force its opponent. Then there took place an action, or rather a cannonade, the result of which is more difficult to explain, perhaps, than any other considerable action of the revolutionary wars. For some hours the Prussian artillery, later reinforced by the Austrian, cannon-aded the French position, having for its central mark the windmill of Valmy, round which the French forces were grouped. At one moment this cannonade took effect upon the limbers and ammunition wagons of the French; there was an explosion which all eye-witnesses have remembered as the chief feature of the firing, and which certainly threw into confusion for some moments the ill-assorted troops under Kellermann's command. At what hour this took place the witnesses who have left us accounts differ to an extraordinary extent. Some will have it at noon, others towards the middle of the afternoon—so difficult is it to have any accurate account of what happens in the heat of an action. At any rate, if not coincidently with this success, at some moment not far removed from it, the Prussian charge was ordered, and it is here that the difficulties of the historian chiefly appear. That charge was never carried home; whether, as some believe, because it was discovered, after it was ordered, to be impossible in the face of the accuracy and intensity of the French fire, or whether, as is more probably the case, because the drenched soil compelled the commanders to abandon the movement after it had begun—whatever the cause may have been, the Prussian force, though admirably disciplined and led, and though advancing in the most exact order, failed to carry out its original purpose. It halted halfway up the slope, and the action remained a mere cannonade without immediate result apparent upon either side.

Nevertheless that result ultimately turned out to be very great, and if we consider its place in history, quite as important as might have been the result of a decisive action. In the first place, the one day's delay which it involved was just more than the calculations of the Allies, with their long impeded line of communications, had allowed for. In the next place, a singular increase in determination and moral force was infused into the disheartened and ill-matched troops of the French commanders by this piece of resistance.

We must remember that the French force upon the whole expected and discounted a defeat, the private soldier especially had no confidence in the result; and to find that at the first action which had been so long threatened and had now at last come, he could stand up to the enemy, produced upon him an exaggerated effect which it would never have had under other circumstances.

Finally, we must recollect that whatever causes had forbidden the Prussian charge forbade on the next day a general advance against the French position. And all the time the sickness in the Prussian camp was rapidly increasing. Even that short check of twenty-four hours made a considerable difference. A further delay of but yet another day, during which the Allied Army could not decide whether to attack at once or to stand as they were, very greatly increased the list of inefficients from illness.

For a whole week of increasing anxiety and increasing inefficiency the Allied Army hung thus, impotent, though they were between the French forces and the capital. Dumouriez ably entertained this hesitation, with all its accumulating dangers for the enemy, by prolonged negotiations, until upon the 30th of September the Prussian and Austrian organisation could stand the strain no longer, and its commanders determined upon retreat. It was the genius of Danton, as we now know, that chiefly organised the withdrawal of what might still have been a dangerous invading force. It is principally due to him that no unwise Jingoism was permitted to claim a trial of strength with the invader, that he was allowed to retire with all his guns, his colours and his train. The retreat was lengthy and unmolested, though watched by the French forces that discreetly shepherded it but were kept tightly in hand from Paris. It was more than three weeks later when the Allied Army, upon which Europe and the French monarchy had counted for an immediate settlement of the Revolution, re-crossed the frontier, and in this doubtful and perhaps inexplicable fashion the first campaign of the European Powers against the Revolution utterly failed.

THREE

Following upon this success, Dumouriez pressed on to what had been, from the first moment of his power at the head of the army, his personal plan—to wit, the invasion of the Low Countries.

To understand why this invasion failed and why Dumouriez thought it might succeed, we must appreciate the military and political situation of the Low Countries at the time. They then formed a very wealthy and cherished portion of the Austrian dominions; they had latterly suffered from deep disaffection culminating in an open revolution, which was due to the Emperor of Austria's narrow and intolerant contempt of religion. From his first foolish policy of persecution and confiscation he had indeed retreated, but the feeling of the people was still strongly opposed to the Government at Vienna. It is remarkable, indeed, and in part due to the pressure of a strongly Protestant and aristocratic state, Holland, to the north of them,

that the people of the Austrian Netherlands retained at that time a peculiar attachment to the Catholic religion. The Revolution was quite as anti-Catholic as the Austrian Emperor, but of the persecution of the latter the Belgians (as we now call them) knew something; that of the former they had not yet learnt to dread. It was, therefore, Dumouriez' calculation that, in invading this province of the Austrian power, he would be fighting in friendly territory. Again, it was separated from the political centre of the empire; it was, therefore, more or less isolated politically, and even for military purposes communication with it was not so easy, unless, indeed, Austria could count on a complete co-operation with Prussia, which Power had been for now so long her ruthless and persistent rival.

Favourable, however, as the circumstances appeared for an invasion, two factors telling heavily against the French had to be counted: the first was the formation of their army, the second the spirit of rebellion against any anti-Catholic Government which had given such trouble to Joseph II.

Of these two factors by far the most important was, of course, the first. If the French forces had been homogeneous, in good spirit, and well trained, they might have held what they won; as a fact, they were most unhomogeneous, great portions of them were ill trained, and, worst of all, there was no consistent theory of subordinate command. Men who imagined that subordinate, that is, regimental, command in an army could be erected from below, and that a fighting force could resemble a somewhat lax and turbulent democracy, marched alongside of and were actually incorporated with old soldiers who had spent their whole careers under an unquestioned discipline, and under a subordinate command which came to them they knew not whence, and as it were by fate. The mere mixture of two such different classes of men in one force would have been bad enough to deal with, but what was worse, the political theories of the day fostered the military error of the new battalions though the politicians dared not interfere with the valuable organisation of the old.

The invasion of the Low Countries began with a great, though somewhat informal and unfruitful success, in the victory of Jemappes. It was the first striking and dramatic decisive action which the French, always of an eager appetite for such news, had been given since between forty and fifty years. The success in America against the English, though brilliantly won and solidly founded, had not presented occasions of this character, and Fontenoy was the last national victory which Paris could remember. Men elderly or old in this autumn of 1792 would have been boys or very young men when Fontenoy was fought. The eager generation of the Revolution, with its military appetites and aptitudes, as yet had hardly expected victory, though victory was ardently desired by them and peculiarly suitable to their temper.

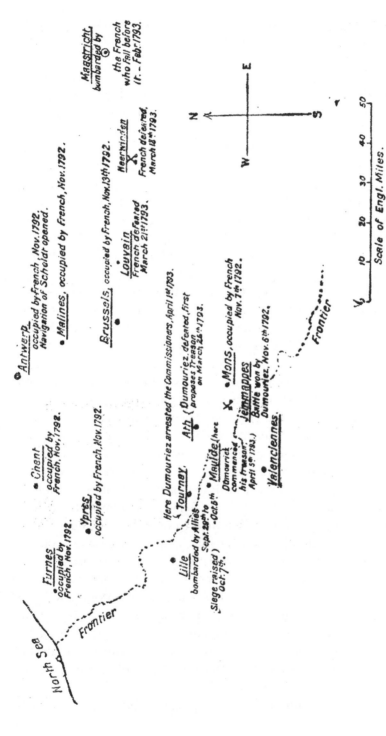

North Sea

Frontier

Furnes
occupied by
French, Nov. 1792.

Ghent
occupied by
French, Nov. 1792.

Ypres
occupied by French, Nov. 1792.

Lille
bombarded by Allies
Sept. 29th to
Oct. 5th

Siege raised
Oct. 7th.

Tournay.

Maulde, (here
Dumouriez
commenced
his treason.
April 5th 1793.)

Ath (Dumouriez, defeated, first
proposes Treason
on March 23rd 1793.

Here Dumouriez arrested the Commissioners, April 1st 1793.

Valenciennes.

Jemmappes
Battle won by
Dumouriez, Nov. 6th 1792.

Mons, occupied by French
Nov. 7th 1792.

Antwerp,
occupied by French, Nov. 1792.
Navigation of Scheldt opened.

Malines, occupied by French, Nov. 1792.

Brussels, occupied by French, Nov. 13th 1792.

Louvain
French defeated
March 21st 1793.

Neerwinden
X
French defeated,
March 18th 1793.

Maastricht
bombarded by
the French
who fall before
it. – Febr. 1793.

Frontier

N
W   E
S

Scale of Engl. Miles.

10   20   30   40   50

Sketch Map of towns occupied by French in 1792 and evacuated in March 1793, with sites of battles
of Jemappes and of Neerwinden, and of Dumouriez' treason.

It may be imagined, therefore, what an effect the news of Jemappes had upon the political world in Paris. The action was fought just below the town of Mons, a few miles over the frontier, and consisted in a somewhat ill-ordered but successful advance across the River Haine. Whether because the Austrians, with an inferior force, attempted to hold too long a line, or because the infantry and even the new French volunteer battalions, as yet untried by fatigue, proved irresistible in the centre of the movement, Jemappes was a victory so complete that the attempts of apologists to belittle it only serve to enhance its character.

Like many another great and apparently decisive action, however, it bore no lasting fruit. Both the factors of which I have spoken above appeared immediately after this success. Belgium was, indeed, over-run by the French, but in their over-running of it with something like eighty thousand men, they made no attempt to spare the traditions or to conciliate the sympathies of the inhabitants. Hardly was Jemappes won when Mons, the neighbouring fortified frontier town, was at once endowed with the whole machinery of revolutionary government. Church property was invaded and occasionally rifled, and the French paper money, the assignats of which we have heard, poured in to disturb and in places to ruin the excellent commercial system upon which Belgium then as now reposedJemappes was fought upon the 6th of November, 1702. Brussels was entered upon the 14th, and throughout that winter the Low Countries lay entirely in the hands of the French. The Commissioners from the Convention, though endowing Belgium with republican institutions, treated it as a conquered country, and before the breaking of spring, the French Parliament voted its annexation to France. This annexation, the determination of the politicians in Paris that the new Belgian Government should be republican and anti-Catholic, the maltreatment of the Church in the occupied country and the increasing ill discipline and lack of cohesion in his army, left Dumouriez in a position which grew more and more difficult as the new year, 1793, advanced. It must be remembered that this moment exactly corresponded with the execution of the King and the consequent declaration of war by or against France in the case of one Power after another throughout Europe. Meanwhile, it was decided, foolishly enough, to proceed from the difficult occupation of Belgium to the still more difficult occupation of Holland, and the siege of Maestricht was planned.

The moment was utterly ill-suited for such a plan. Every Executive in the civilised world was coalescing openly or secretly, directly or indirectly, against the revolutionary Government. The first order to retreat came upon the 8th of March, when the siege of Maestricht was seen to be impossible, and when the great forces of the Allies were gathered again to attempt what was to be the really serious attack upon the Revolution: something far more dangerous, something which much more nearly achieved success, than the march of the comparatively small force which had been checked at Valmy.

For ten days the French retreat continued, when, upon the 18th of March, Dumouriez risked battle at Neerwinden. His army was defeated.

The defeat was not disastrous, the retreat was continued in fairly good order, but a civilian population understands nothing besides the words defeat and victory; it can appreciate a battle, not a campaign. The news of the defeat, coming at a moment of crisis in the politics of Paris, was decisive; it led to grave doubts of Dumouriez' loyalty to the revolutionary Government, it shattered his popularity with those who had continued to believe in him, while the general himself could not but believe that the material under his command was rapidly deteriorating. Before the end of the month the army had abandoned all its conquests, and Valenciennes, in French territory, was reached upon the 27th. The dash upon Belgium had wholly failed.

At this moment came one of those political acts which so considerably disturb any purely military conspectus of the revolutionary wars. Dumouriez, at the head of his army, which, though in retreat and defeated, was still intact, determined upon what posterity has justly called treason, but what to his own mind must have seemed no more than statesmanship. He proposed an understanding with the enemy and a combined march upon Paris to restore the monarchical government, and put an end to what seemed to him, as a soldier, a perfectly hopeless situation. He certainly believed it impossible for the French army, in the welter of 1793, to defeat the invader. He saw his own life in peril merely because he was defeated. He had no toleration for the rising enthusiasm or delirium of the political theory which had sent him out, and, even before he had reached French territory, his negotiations with Coburg, the Austrian commander, had begun. They lasted long. Dumouriez agreed to put the frontier fortresses of the French into the hands of the enemy as a guarantee and a pledge; and on the 5th of April all was ready for the alliance of the two armed forces.

But just as the treason of Dumouriez is, in the military sense, abnormal and disturbing to any general conspectus of the campaign, so was the action of his army.

The doubtful point of a general command which is political in nature, and may be unpopular with the rank and file, lies, of course, in the attitude of the commanders of units, and these unanimously refused to obey the orders of their chief. It was known that Dumouriez had been summoned to the bar of the Convention, which body had sent commissioners to apprehend him. He had arrested the commissioners, and had handed them over as hostages and prisoners to Coburg. So far from Dumouriez upon the critical day handing over his force to the enemy, or constituting it a part of an allied army to march upon the capital, he was compelled to fly upon the 8th of April; all that disappeared with him, counting many who later deserted back again to the French colours, was less than a thousand men—and these foreign mercenaries.

The consequence of this strange passage upon the political history of the time we have already seen. Its consequence upon the military history of it was indirect but profound. The French forces, such as they were, were still intact, but no general officer could in future be trusted by Paris, and the stimulus which nations in the critical moments of invasion and of danger during foreign war seek in patriotism, in the offering of a high wage to the men and of honours and fortunes to their commanders, was now sought by the French in the singular, novel and abnormal experiment of the Terror. Command upon the frontier throughout 1793 and the first part of 1794, during the critical fourteen months, that is, which decided the fate of the Revolution, and which turned the tide of arms in favour of the French, was a task accomplished under the motive power of capital punishment. A blunder was taken as a proof of treason, and there lay over the ordering of every general movement the threat of the guillotine.

What we have now to follow is somewhat over a year of a struggle thus abnormally organised upon the French side, and finally successful through the genius of a great organiser, once a soldier, now a politician, Carnot. The French succeeded by the unshakable conviction which permitted the political leaders to proceed to all extremity in their determination to save the Revolution; by the peculiar physical powers of endurance which their army displayed, and finally, of course, by certain accidents—for accident will always be a determining factor in war.

The spring of 1793, the months of April and May, form the first crisis of the revolutionary war. The attack about to be delivered is universal, and seems absolutely certain to succeed. With the exception of the rush at Jemappes, where less than thirty thousand Austrians were broken through by a torrent superior in numbers (though even there obviously ill-organised), no success had attended the revolutionary armies. Their condition was, even to the eye of the layman, bad, and to the eye of the expert hopeless. There was no unity apparent in direction, there were vast lesions in the discipline of the ranks like great holes torn in some rotten fabric. Even against the forces already mobilised against it, it had proved powerless, and it might be taken for granted that by an act more nearly resembling police work than a true campaign, the Allies would reach Paris and something resembling the old order be soon restored. What remains is to follow the process by which this expectation was disappointed.

The situation at this moment can best be understood by a glance at the sketch map on p. 110. Two great French advances had been made in the winter of 1792–93; the one a northern advance, which we have just detailed, the over-running of Belgium; the other an eastern advance right up to the Rhine and to the town of Mayence. Both had failed. The failure in Belgium, culminating in the treason of Dumouriez, has been read. On the Rhine (where Mayence had been annexed by the French Parliament just as Belgium had been) the active hostility of the population and the gathering of the organised forces of the Allies had the same effect as had been produced in the Low Countries.

It was on March 21, 1793, that the Prussians crossed the Rhine at Bacharach, and within that week the French commander, Custine, began to fall back. On the first of April he was back again in French territory, leaving the garrison of Mayence, somewhat over twenty thousand men, to hold out as best it could; a fortnight later the Prussians had surrounded the town and the siege had begun.

On the north-eastern front, stretching from the Ardennes to the sea, a similar state of things was developing. There, a barrier of fortresses stood between the Allies and Paris, and a series of sieges corresponding to the siege of Mayence in the east had to be undertaken. At much the same time as the investment of Mayence, on April 9, the first step in this military task was taken by the Allies moving in between the fortress of Condé and the fortress of Valenciennes. Thenceforward it was the business of the Austrians under Coburg, with the Allies that were to reach him, to reduce the frontier fortresses one by one, and when his communications were thus secure, to march upon Paris.

It is here necessary for the reader unacquainted with military history to appreciate two points upon which not a little of contemporary historical writing may mislead him. The first is that both in the Rhine valley and on the Belgian frontier the forces of the Allies in their numbers and their organisation were conceived to be overwhelming. The second is that no competent commander on the spot would have thought of leaving behind him the garrison of even one untaken fortress. It is important to insist upon these points, because the political passions roused by the Revolution are still so strong that men can hardly write of it without prejudice and bias, and two errors continually present in these descriptions of the military situation in the spring of 1793, are, first, that the Allies were weakened by the Polish question, which was then active, and secondly, that the delay of their commanders before the French fortresses was unnecessary.

Both these propositions are put forward with the object of explaining the ultimate defeat of the enemies of the Revolution: both, however great the authority behind them, are unhistorical and worthless. The French success was a military success due to certain military factors both of design and accident, which will appear in what follows. The Allies played their part as all the art of war demanded it to be played; they were ultimately defeated, not from the commission of any such gross and obvious error in policy or strategy as historians with too little comprehension of military affairs sometimes pretend, but from the military superiority of their opponents.

It is true that the Polish question (that is the necessity the Austrian and Prussian Governments were each under of watching that the other was not lessened in importance by the approaching annexations of further Polish territory with the consequent jealousy and mistrust that arose from this between Austria and Prussia) was a very important feature of the moment. But it is bad military history to pretend that this affected the military situation on the Rhine or in the Netherlands.

Every campaign is conditioned by its political object. The political object in this case was to march upon and to occupy Paris. The political object of a campaign once determined, the size and the organisation of the enemy are calculated and a certain force is brought against it. No much larger force is brought than is necessary: to act in such a fashion would be in military art what paying two or three times the price of an article would be in commerce. The forces of the Allies upon the Rhine and in the Netherlands were, in the opinion of every authority of the time, amply sufficient for their purpose; and more than sufficient: so much more than sufficient that the attitude of that military opinion which had to meet the attack—to wit, the professional military opinion of the French republican soldiers, was that the situation was desperate, nor indeed was it attempted to be met save by a violent and, as it were, irrational enthusiasm.

The second point, the so-called "delay" involved in the sieges undertaken by the Allies, proves, when it is put forward, an insufficient acquaintance with contemporary conditions. Any fortress with a considerable garrison left behind untaken would have meant the destruction of the Austrian or Prussian communications, and their destruction at a moment when the Austrian and Prussian forces were actually advancing over a desperately hostile country. Moreover, when acting against forces wholly inferior in discipline and organisation, an untaken fortress is a refuge which one must take peculiar pains to destroy. To throw himself into such a refuge will always stand before the commander of those inferior forces as a last resource. It is a refuge which he will certainly avail himself of ultimately, if it is permitted to him. And when he has so availed himself of it, it means the indefinite survival of an armed organisation in the rear of the advancing invaders. We must conclude, if we are to understand this critical campaign which changed the history of the world, that Coburg did perfectly right in laying siege to one fortress after another before he began what every one expected to be the necessarily successful advance on Paris. The French despair, as one town after another surrendered, is an amply sufficient proof of the excellence of his judgment.

We approach the military problem of 1793, therefore, with the following two fields clear before us:—

1. In the north-east an advance on Paris, the way to which is blocked by a quadrilateral of fortresses: Mons, Maubeuge, Condé, and Valenciennes, with the subsidiary stronghold of Lequesnoy in the neighbourhood of the last. Mons has been in Austrian hands since Dumouriez' retreat; Condé is just cut off from Valenciennes by Coburg's advance, but has not fallen; Valenciennes and the neighbouring Lequesnoy are still intact, and so is Maubeuge. All must be reduced before the advance on Paris can begin. Behind these fortresses is a French army incapable as yet of attacking Coburg's command with

any hope of success. Such is the position in the last fortnight of April.

2. Meanwhile, on the Rhine the French garrison in Mayence is besieged; Custine, the French commander in that quarter, has fallen back on the French town of Landau, and is drawing up what are known in history as the Lines of Weissembourg. The accompanying sketch map explains their importance. Reposing upon the two obstacles of the river on the right and the mountains on the left, they fulfilled precisely the same functions as a fortress; and those functions we have just described. Until these lines were carried, the whole of Alsace may be regarded as a fortress defended by the mountains and the river on two sides, and by the Lines of Weissembourg on the third.

A reader unacquainted with military history may ask why the obstruction was not drawn upon the line of the Prussian advance on Paris. The answer is that the presence of a force behind fortifications anywhere in the neighbourhood of a line of communication is precisely equivalent to an obstacle lying right upon those lines. For no commander can go forward along the line of his advance and leave a large undestroyed force close to one side of that line, and so situated that it can come out when he has passed and cut off his communications; for it is by communications that an army lives, especially when it is marching in hostile country.

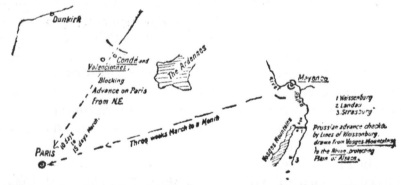

Strategic situation in early summer of 1793. Mayence besieged, Condé and Valenciennes about to be besieged. Conditions of the double advance on Paris.

Custine, therefore, behind his Lines of Weissembourg, and the besieged garrison in Mayence, correspond to the barrier of fortresses on the north-east and delayed the advance of the Prussians under Wurmser and Brunswick from the Rhine, just as Condé, Valenciennes, and Maubeuge prevented the advance of Coburg on the north-east. Such in general was the situation upon the eastern frontier at the end of that month of April, 1793.

FOUR

Let us first follow the development of the northern position. It will be remembered that all Europe was at war against the French. The Austrians had for allies Dutch troops which joined them at this moment, and certain English and Hanoverian troops under the Duke of York who also joined them.

At this moment, when Coburg found himself in increasing strength, a tentative French attack upon him was delivered and failed. Dampierre, who was in command of all this French "Army of the North," was killed, and Custine was sent to replace him. The Army of the North did not, as perhaps it should have done, concentrate into one body to meet Coburg's threatened advance; it was perpetually attempting diversions which were useless because its strength was insufficient. Now it feinted upon the right towards Namur, now along the sea coast on the left; and these diversions failed in their object. Before the end of the month, Coburg, to give himself elbow room, as it were, for the sieges which he was preparing, compelled the main French force to retreat to a position well behind Valenciennes. It was immediately after this success of Coburg's that Custine arrived to take command on the Belgian frontier, his place on the Rhine being taken by Houchard.

Custine was a very able commander, but a most unlucky one. His plan was the right one: to concentrate all the French forces (abandoning the Rhine) and so form an army sufficient to cope with Coburg's. The Government would not meet him in this, and he devoted himself immediately to the reorganisation of the Army of the North alone. The month of June and half of July was taken up in that task.

Meanwhile, the Austrian siege work had begun, and Condé was the first object of its attention. Upon July 10 Condé fell. Meanwhile Custine had been recalled to Paris, and Valenciennes was invested. Custine was succeeded by Kilmaine, a general of Irish extraction, who maintained his position for but a short time, and was unable while he maintained it to do anything. The forces of the Allies continually increased. The number at Coburg's disposal free from the business of besieging Valenciennes was already larger than the force required for that purpose. And yet another fifteen thousand Hessian troops marched in while the issue of that siege was in doubt. This great advantage in numbers permitted him to get rid of the main French force that was still present in front of him, though not seriously annoying him.

This force lay due south-west of Valenciennes, and about a day's march distant. He depended for the capture of it upon his English and Hanoverian Allies under the Duke of York, but that general's march failed. The distance was too much for his troops in the hot summer weather, and the French were able to retreat behind the line of the Scarpe and save their army intact.

The Duke of York's talents have been patriotically exaggerated in many a treatise. He always failed: and this was among the most signal of his failures.

Kilmaine had hardly escaped from York, drawn up his army behind the Scarpe and put it into a position of safety when he in his turn was deprived of the command, and Houchard was taken from the Rhine just as Custine had been, and put at the head of the Army of the North. Before the main French army had taken up this position of safety, Valenciennes had fallen. It fell on the 28th of July, and its fall, inevitable though it was and, as one may say, taken for granted by military opinion, was much the heaviest blow yet delivered. Nothing of importance remained to block the march of the Armies of the Allies, save Maubeuge.

At about the same moment occurred three very important changes in the general military situation, which the reader must note if he is to understand what follows.

The first was the sudden serious internal menace opposed to the Republican Government; the second was the advent of Carnot to power; the third was the English diversion upon Dunquerque.

The serious internal menace which the Government of the Republic had to face was the widespread rebellion which has been dealt with in the earlier part of this book. The action of the Paris Radicals against the Girondins had raised whole districts in the provinces. Marseilles, which had shown signs of disaffection since April, and had begun to raise a local reactionary force, revolted. So did Bordeaux, Nîmes, and other great southern towns. Lyons had risen at the end of May and had killed the Jacobin mayor of the town in the period between the fall of Condé and that of Valenciennes. The troop which Marseilles had raised against the Republic was defeated in the field only the day before Valenciennes fell, but the great seaport was still unoccupied by the forces of the Government. The Norman march upon Paris had also failed between those two dates, the fall of Condé and the fall of Valenciennes. The Norman bark had proved worse than the Norman bite; but the force was so neighbouring to the capital that it took a very large place in the preoccupations of the time. The Vendean revolt, though its triumphant advance was checked before Nantes a fortnight before the fall of Condé, was still vigorous, and the terrible reprisals against it were hardly begun. Worst of all, or at least, worst perhaps, after the revolt of Lyons, was the defection of Toulon. Toulon rose two days before the fall of Valenciennes, and was prepared to hand itself over (as at last it did hand itself over) to occupation by the English fleet.The dates thus set in their order may somewhat confuse the reader, and I will therefore summarise the general position of the internal danger thus: A man in the French camp on the Scheldt, listening to the guns before Valenciennes fifteen miles away, and hourly expecting their silence as a signal that the city had surrendered, would have heard by one post after another how Marseilles still held out against the Government; how the counter-attack against the successful Vendeans had but doubtfully begun (all July was full of disasters in that quarter); how Lyons was furiously successful in her rebellion and had dared to put to death the Republican mayor of the town; and that the great arsenal and port at Toulon, the Portsmouth of France upon the Mediterranean, had sickened of the Government and was about to admit the English fleet. His only comfort would have been to hear that the Norman march on Paris had failed—but he would still be under the impression of it and of the murder of Marat by a Norman woman.

There is the picture of that sudden internal struggle which coincides with this moment of the revolutionary war, the moment of the fall of Condé and of Valenciennes, and the exposure of the frontier.

The second point, the advent of Carnot into the Committee of Public Safety, which has already been touched upon in the political part of this work, has so preponderating a military significance that we must consider it here also.

The old Committee of Public Safety, it will be remembered, reached the end of its legal term on July 10. It was the Committee which the wisdom of Danton had controlled. The members elected to the new Committee did not include Carnot, but the military genius of this man was already public. He came of that strong middle class which is the pivot upon which the history of modern Europe turns; a Burgundian with lineage, intensely republican, he had been returned to the Convention and had voted for the death of the King; a sapper before the Revolution, and one thoroughly well grounded in his arm and in general reading of military things, he had been sent by the Convention to the Army of the North on commission, he had seen its weakness and had watched its experiments. Upon his return he was not immediately selected for the post in which he was to transform the revolutionary war. It was not until the 14th of August that he was given a temporary place upon the Committee which his talents very soon made permanent. He was given the place merely as a stopgap to the odious and incompetent fanatic, Saint-André, who was for the moment away on mission. But from the day of his admission his superiority in military affairs was so incontestable that he was virtually a dictator therein, and his first action after the general lines of organisation had been laid down by him was to impose upon the frontier armies the necessity of concentration. He introduced what afterwards Napoleon inherited from him, the tactical venture of "all upon one throw."

It must be remembered that Carnot's success did not lie in any revolutionary discovery in connection with the art of war, but rather in that vast capacity for varied detail which marks the organiser, and in an intimate sympathy with the national character. He understood the contempt for parade, the severity or brutality of discipline, the consciousness of immense powers of endurance which are in the Frenchman when he becomes a soldier;—and he made use of this understanding of his.

It must be further remembered that this powerful genius had behind him in these first days of his activity the equally powerful genius of Danton; for it was Danton and he who gave practical shape to that law of conscription by which the French Revolution suddenly increased its armed forces by nearly half a million of men, restored the Roman tradition, and laid the foundation of the armed system on which Europe to-day depends. With Carnot virtually commander-in-chief of all the armies, and enabled to impose his decisions in particular upon that Army of the North which he had studied so recently as a commissioner, the second factor of the situation I am describing is comprehended.

The third, as I have said, was the English diversion upon Dunquerque.

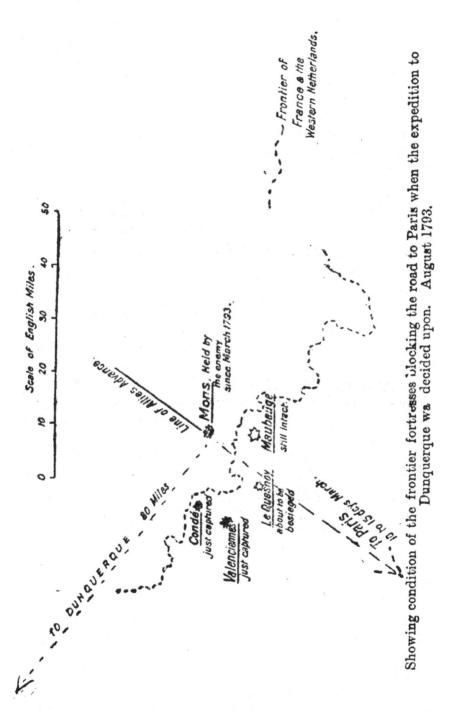

Showing condition of the frontier fortresses blocking the road to Paris when the expedition to Dunquerque was decided upon.   August 1793.

Scale of English Miles.

0   10   20   30   40   50

TO DUNQUERQUE —— 80 Miles

Line of Allies Advance

Condé
just captured

Valenciennes
just captured

Le Quesnoy
about to be
besieged

Mons, Held by
The enemy
since March 1793.

Maubeuge
still intact.

To Paris
13 to 15 days March.

Frontier of
France & the
Western Netherlands.

The subsequent failure of the Allies has led to bitter criticism of this movement. Had the Allies not failed, history would have treated it as its contemporaries treated it. The forces of the Allies on the north-eastern frontier were so great and their confidence so secure—especially after the fall of Valenciennes—that the English proposal to withdraw their forces for the moment from Coburg's and to secure Dunquerque, was not received with any destructive criticism. Eighteen battalions and fourteen squadrons of the Imperial forces were actually lent to the Duke of York for this expedition. What is more, even after that diversion failed, the plan was fixed to begin again when the last of the other fortresses should have fallen: so little was the English plan for the capture of the seaport disfavoured by the commander-in-chief of the Allies.

That diversion on Dunquerque turned out, however, to be an error of capital importance. The attempt to capture the city utterly failed, and the victory which accompanied its repulsion had upon the French that indefinable but powerful moral effect which largely contributed to their future successes.

The accompanying sketch map will explain the position. Valenciennes and Condé have fallen; Lequesnoy, the small fortress subsidiary to Valenciennes, has not yet been attacked but comes next in the series, when the moment was judged propitious for the detachment of the Anglo-Hanoverian force with a certain number of Imperial Allies to march to the sea.

It must always be remembered by the reader of history that military situations, like the situations upon a chess board, rather happen than are designed; and the situation which developed at the end of September upon the extreme north and west of the line which the French were attempting to hold against the Allies was strategically of this nature. When the Duke of York insisted upon a division of the forces of the Allies and an attack upon Dunquerque, no living contemporary foresaw disaster.

Coburg, indeed, would have preferred the English to remain with him, and asked them to do so, but he felt in no sort of danger through their temporary absence, nor, as a matter of fact, was he in any danger through it.

Again, though the positions which the Duke of York took up when he arrived in front of Dunquerque were bad, neither his critics at home, nor any of his own subordinates, nor any of the enemy, perceived fully how bad they were. It was, as will presently be seen, a sort of drift, bad luck combined with bad management, which led to this British disaster, and (what was all-important for the conduct of the war) to the first success in a general action which the French had to flatter and encourage themselves with during all that fatal summer.

The Duke of York separated his force from that of Coburg just before the middle of August; besides the British, who were not quite 7,000 strong, 11,000 Austrians, over 10,000 Hanoverians and 7,000 Hessians were under his command. The total force, therefore, was nearly 37,000 strong. No one could imagine that, opposed by such troops as the French were able to put into line, and marching against such wretched defences as those of Dunquerque then were, the Duke's army had not a perfectly easy task before it; and the plan, which was to take Dunquerque and upon the return to join the Austrian march on Paris, was reasonable and feasible.

It is important that the reader should firmly seize this and not read history backward from future events.

Certain faults are to be observed in the first conduct of the march. It began on the 15th of August, proceeding from Marchiennes to Menin, and at the outset displayed that deplorable lack of marching power which the Duke of York's command had shown throughout the campaign.* From Marchiennes to Tourcoing is a long day's march: it took the Duke of York four days; and, take the march altogether, nine days were spent in covering less than forty miles. In the course of that march, the British troops had an opportunity of learning to despise their adversary: they found at Linselles, upon the flank of their advance, a number of undisciplined boys who broke the moment the Guards were upon them, and whose physical condition excited the ridicule of their assailants. The army proceeded after this purposeless and unfruitful skirmish to the neighbourhood of the sea coast, and the siege of Dunquerque was undertaken under conditions which will be clear to the reader from the following sketch map.

The date of the 20th of August must first be fixed in the mind: on that date the army which was to take Dunquerque was separated into

---

* Incidentally it should be noted how true it is that this supreme military quality is a matter of organisation rather than of the physical power of troops; in the Napoleonic wars the marching power of the English troops was often proved exceptional, and perhaps the greatest of all feats accomplished by a small body was that of the Light Brigade marching to the succour of Wellington at Talavera.

its two component parts. The first, under the Duke of York, was to attack the town itself; the second, under the aged Austrian general, Freytag, was to watch the movement of any approaching enemy and to cover the force which was besieging the town. Two days later, the Duke of York was leaving Furnes, which he had made his base for the advance, and Freytag had with the greatest ease brushed the French posts—mainly of volunteers—from before him, and was beginning to take up the flanking positions south and east of Bergues which covered the siege of Dunquerque.

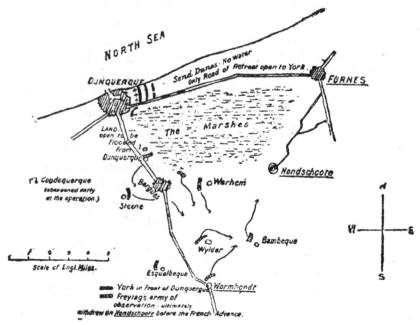

Operations round Dunquerque.   September 1793.

Two days later again, on August 24, Freytag had occupied Wormhoudt and Esquelbecque, capturing guns by the dozen, doing pretty well what he would with the French outposts, and quite surrounding the town of Bergues. Wilder was his headquarters. On the same day, the 24th, the Duke of York had with the greatest ease driven in the advanced posts of the French before Dunquerque, and shut up the enemy within the town, while he formed his besieging force outside of it, entrenched in a position which he had chosen beforehand, reposing upon the sea at his right, his left on the village of Tetteghem. He was then about 3,000 yards from the fortifications at Dunquerque.

Such was the situation upon the dawn of the 25th, when everything was ready for active operations. And here the reader must look upon the map for what ultimately proved the ruin of the situation.

Supposing Freytag round Bergues in the position which the map shows; the Duke of York in front of Dunquerque as the map also shows him; the two forces are in touch across the road and the belt of country which unites Bergues and Dunquerque. The covering army and the besieging force which it covers are each a wing of one combined body; each communicates with the other, each can support the other at the main point of effort, and though between the one and the other eastward there stretches a line of marshy country—the "meres" which the map indicates—yet a junction between the two forces exists westward of these, and the two armies can co-operate by the Bergues-Dunquerque road.

A factor which the Duke of York may have neglected was the power of flooding all that flat country round, the road which the French in Dunquerque, being in possession of the sluices, possessed. They used it at once: they drowned the low lands to the south of Dunquerque, upon the very day when the last dispositions of the attacking force were completed. But more important—and never yet explained—was the Austrians' abandonment of Coudequerque. By this error, the main road itself, standing above the flood, was lost, and from being one strong army the force of the Allies became two weak ones. Communication was no longer possible between the Duke of York's and Freytag's territories, and it was of this separation that the French, in spite of their deplorable organisation and more deplorable personnel, took advantage.

They took advantage of it slowly. Houchard gathered altogether forty thousand men near Cassel, but it was ten days before they could be concentrated. It must again be insisted upon and repeated that, large as the number was—it was four times as great as Freytag's now isolated force—Houchard's command was made up of men quite two-thirds of whom were hardly soldiers: volunteers both new and recent, ill-trained conscripts and so forth. There was no basis of discipline, hardly any power to enforce it; the men had behaved disgracefully in all the affairs of outposts, they had been brushed away contemptuously by the small Austrian force from every position they had held. With all his numerical superiority the attempt which Houchard was about to make was very hazardous: and Houchard was a hesitating and uncertain commander. Furthermore, of the forty thousand men one quarter at least remained out of action through the ineptitude and political terror of Dumesny, Houchard's lieutenant upon the right.

It was upon the 6th of September that the French advance began along the whole line; it was a mere pushing in of inferior numbers by superior numbers, the superior numbers perpetually proving themselves inferior to the Austrians in military value. Thus, the capture of old Freytag himself in a night skirmish was at once avenged by the storming of the village near which he had been caught, and he was re-taken. In actual fighting and force for force, Houchard's command found nothing to encourage it during these first operations.

The Austrians in falling back concentrated and were soon one compact body: to attack and dislodge it was the object of the French advance, but an object hardly to be attained.

What happened was not only the unexpected success of this advance, but the gaining by the French of the first decisive action in the long series which was to terminate twenty years later at Leipsic.

The army of Freytag fell back upon the village of Hondschoote and stood there in full force upon the morning of Sunday, the 8th of September. Houchard attacked it with a force greatly lessened but still double that of the defenders. So conspicuous, however, was the superiority of the Austrian regulars over the French raw troops and volunteers that during this morning of the 8th the result was still doubtful. By the afternoon, however, the work was done, and the enemy were in a retreat which might easily have been turned into a rout. A glance at the map will show that Houchard, had he possessed the initiative common to so many of his contemporaries, might at once have driven the numerically inferior and heavily defeated force (it had lost one-third of its men) to the right, and proceeded himself to cut the communications of the Duke of York and to destroy his army, which lay packed upon the waterless sand dunes where the village of Malo-les-Bains now stands. Houchard hesitated; Freytag escaped; the Duke of York, abandoning his siege-pieces to the number of forty and much of his heavy baggage, retreated precipitately through the night to Furnes, right across the front of the French army, and escaped destruction.

The Battle of Hoondschoote, therefore, as it is called, raised the siege of Dunquerque. It was, as I have said, the first successful decisive action which the Revolution could count since the moment of its extreme danger and the opening of the general European war. But it was nothing like what it might have been had Houchard been willing to risk a hardy stroke. Houchard was therefore recalled, condemned to death, and executed by the Committee of Public Safety, whose pitiless despotism was alone capable of saving the nation. He remains the single example of a general officer who has suffered death for military incompetence after the gaining of a victory, and his execution is an excellent example of the way in which the military temper of the Committee, and particularly of Carnot, refused to consider any factor in the war save those that make for military success.

Carnot and the Committee had no patience with the illusions which a civilian crowd possesses upon mere individual actions: what they saw was the campaign as a whole, and they knew that Houchard had left the armies opposite him intact.

Perhaps his execution was made more certain by the continuance of bad news from that more important point of the frontier—the direct line of Austrian advance upon Paris. Here, already, Valenciennes had fallen two months before, and Condé also. Lequesnoy, the third point of the barrier line, capitulated on the 11th of September, and the news of that capitulation reached Paris immediately after the news of Hondschoote. No fortress was now left between the Allies and the capital but Maubeuge. Coburg marched upon it at once.

Not only had he that immense superiority in the quality of his troops which must be still insisted upon, but numerically also he was three to one when, on the 28th of September, at dawn, he crossed the Sambre above and below Maubeuge, and by noon of that day had contained the French army in that neighbourhood within the lines of the fortress.

The situation was critical in the extreme: Maubeuge was ill prepared to stand siege; it was hardly provisioned; its garrison was of varied and, on the whole, of bad quality. In mere victuals it could stand out for but a few days, and, worst of all, it had behind it the continued example of necessary and fatal surrenders which had marked the whole summer. The orders of the Committee of Public Safety to its commander were terse: "Your head shall answer for Maubeuge." After the receipt of that message no more came through the lines.

The reader, if he be unaccustomed to military history, does well to note that in every action and in every campaign there is some one factor of position or of arms or of time which explains the result. Each has a pivot or hinge, as it were, upon which the whole turns. It was now upon Maubeuge that the revolutionary war thus depended. At risk of oversimplifying a complex story, I would lay this down as the prime condition for the understanding of the early revolutionary wars: had Maubeuge fallen, the road to Paris lay open and the trick was done*—and here we must consider again the effect in the field of Carnot's genius.

In the first place, he had provided numbers not on paper, but in reality; the Committee, through a decree of the Assembly, had despotically "requisitioned" men, animals, vehicles and supplies. The levy was a reality. Mere numbers then raw, but increasing, had begun to pour into the north-east. It was they that had told at Hoondschoote, it was they that were to tell in front of Maubeuge.

Secondly, as the Committee supplied the necessary initiative, Carnot supplied the necessary personality of war. His own will and own brain could come to one decision in one moment, and did so. It was he, as we shall see, who won the critical action. He chose Jourdan, a man whose quaint military career we must reluctantly leave aside in so brief a study as this, but at any rate an amateur, and put him in Houchard's command over the Army of the Northern Frontier, and that command was extended from right away beyond the Ardennes to the sea. He ordered (and Jourdan obeyed) the concentration of men from all down that lengthy line to the right and the left upon one point, Guise. To leave the rest of the frontier weak was a grave risk only to be excused by very rapid action and success: both these were to follow. The concentration was effected in four days. Troops from the extreme north could not come in time. The furthest called upon

---

* I must not, in fairness to the reader, neglect the great mass of opinion, from Jomini to Mr. Fortescue's classic work upon the British Army, which lays it down that the Allies had but to mask the frontier fortresses and to advance their cavalry rapidly along the Paris road. Historical hypothesis can never be more than a matter of judgment, but I confess that this view has always seemed to me to ignore—as purely military historians and especially foreign ones might well ignore—the social condition of "'93." Cavalry is the weakest of all arms with which to deal with sporadic, unorganised, but determined resistance. To pass through the densely populated country of the Paris road may be compared to the forcing of an open town, and cavalry can never be relied upon for *that*. As for the army moving as a whole without a perfect security in its communications, the matter need not even be discussed; and it must further be remembered that, the moment such an advance began, an immediate concentration from the north would have fallen upon the ill-guarded lines of supply. It may be taken that Coburg knew his business when he sat down before this, the last of the fortresses.

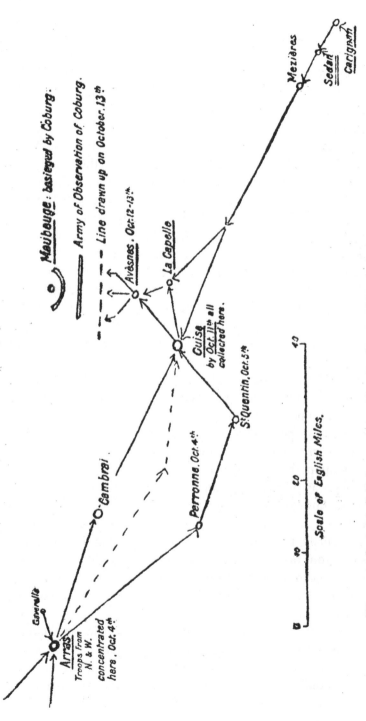

The rapid eight days' concentration in front of Maubeuge. October 1793.

Maubeuge: besieged by Coburg.
——— Army of Observation of Coburg.
– – – Line drawn up on October 13th

Gavrelle

Arras
Troops from N. & W. concentrated here. Oct. 4th

Cambrai

Perronne. Oct. 4th

St Quentin, Oct. 5th

Guise by Oct. 11th all collected here.

Avesnes. Oct. 12-13th

La Capelle

Mezières

Sedan

Carignan

Scale of English Miles.
0   10   20   30

were beyond Arras, with sixty-five miles of route between them and Guise. This division (which shall be typical of many), not quite eight thousand strong, left on receiving orders in the morning of the 3rd of October and entered Guise in the course of the 6th. The rate of marching and the synchrony of these movements of imperfect troops should especially be noted by any one who would understand how the Revolution succeeded.

A second division of over thirteen thousand men followed along the parallel road, with a similar time table. From the other end of his line, a detachment under Beauregard, just over four thousand men, was called up from the extreme right. It will serve as a typical example upon the eastern side of this lightning concentration. It had been gathered near Carignan, a town full fourteen miles beyond Sedan. It picked up reinforcements on the way and marched into Fourmies upon the 11th, after covering just seventy miles in the three and a half days. With its arrival the concentration was complete, and not a moment too soon, for the bombardment of Maubeuge was about to begin. From the 11th to the 15th of October the army was advanced and drawn up in line, a day's march in front of Guise, with its centre at Avesnes and facing the covering army of Coburg, which lay entrenched upon a long wooded crest with the valley of the Sambre upon its right and the village of Wattignies, on a sort of promontory of high land, upon its left.

The Austrian position was reconnoitred upon the 14th. Upon the 15th the general attack was delivered and badly repelled. When darkness fell upon that day few in the army could have believed that Maubeuge was succourable—and it was a question of hours.

Carnot, however, sufficiently knew the virtues as the vices of his novel troops, the troops of the great levy, stiffened with a proportion of regulars, to attempt an extraordinary thing. He marched eight thousand from his left and centre, over to his right during the night, and in the morning of the 16th his right, in front of the Austrian left at Wattignies had, by this conversion, become far the strongest point of the whole line.

A dense mist had covered the end of this operation as the night had covered its inception, and that mist endured until nearly midday. The Austrians upon the heights had no hint of the conversion, and Wattignies was only held by three regiments. If they expected a renewed attack at all, they can only have expected it in the centre, or even upon the left where the French had suffered most the day before.

Initiative in war is essentially a calculation of risk, and with high initiative the risk is high. What Carnot gambled upon (for Jourdan was against the experiment) when he moved those young men through the night, was the possibility of getting active work out of them after a day's furious action, the forced marches of the preceding week and on top of it all a sleepless night of further marching. Most of the men who were prepared to charge on the French right as the day broadened and the mist lifted on that 16th of October, had been on foot for thirty hours. The charge was delivered, and was successful. The unexpected numbers thus concentrated under Wattignies carried that extreme position, held the height, and arrived, therefore, on the flank of the whole Austrian line, which, had not the effort of the aggressors exhausted them, would have been rolled up in its whole length. As it was, the Austrians retreated unmolested and in good order across the Sambre. The siege of Maubeuge was raised; and the next day the victorious French army entered the fortress.

Thus was successfully passed the turning-point of the revolutionary wars.

Two months later the other gate of the country was recovered. In the moment when Maubeuge was relieved, the enemy had pierced the lines of Wissembourg. It is possible that an immediate and decisive understanding among the Allies might then have swept all Alsace; but such an understanding was lacking. The disarrayed "Army of the Rhine" was got into some sort of order, notably through the enthusiasm of Hoche and the silent control of Pichegru. At the end of November the Prussians stood on the defensive at Kaiserslautern. Hoche hammered at them for three days without success. What really turned the scale was the floods of men and material that the levy and the requisitioning were pouring in. Just before Christmas the enemy evacuated Haguenau. Landau they still held; but a decisive action fought upon Boxing Day, a true soldiers' battle, determined by the bayonet, settled the fate of the Allies on this point. The French entered Wissembourg again, and Landau was relieved after a siege of four months and a display of tenacity which had done not a little to turn the tide of the war.

Meanwhile the news had come in that the last of the serious internal rebellions was crushed. Toulon had been re-captured, the English fleet driven out; the town, the harbour and the arsenal had fallen into the hands of the French largely through the science of a young major of artillery (not captain: I have discussed the point elsewhere), Bonaparte, and this had taken place a week before the relief of Landau. The last confused horde of La Vendée had been driven from the walls of Granville in Normandy, to which it had erred and drifted rather than retreated. At Mans on the 13th of December it was cut to pieces, and at Savenay on the 23rd, three days before the great victory in Alsace, it was destroyed. A long peasant-and-bandit struggle, desperate yet hardly to be called guerilla, continued through the next year behind the hedges of Lower Brittany and of Vendée, but the danger to the State and to the Revolution was over. The year 1793 ended, therefore, with the complete relief of the whole territory of the Republic, save a narrow strip upon the Belgian frontier, complete domination of it by its Cæsar, the Committee of Public Safety; with two-thirds of a million of men under arms, and the future of the great experiment apparently secure.

The causes of the wonder have been discussed, and will be discussed indefinitely. Primarily, they resided in the re-creation of a strong central power; secondly, in the combination of vast numbers and of a reckless spirit of sacrifice. The losses on the National side were perpetually and heavily superior to those of the Allies—in Alsace they had been three to one; and we shall better understand the duel when we appreciate that in the short eight years between the opening of the war and the triumph of Napoleon at Marengo, there had fallen in killed and wounded, on the French side, over seven hundred thousand men.

FIVE

The story of 1794 is but the consequence of what we have just read. It was the little belt or patch upon the Belgian frontier which was still in the hands of the enemy that determined the nature of the campaign.

It was not until spring that the issue was joined. The Emperor of Austria reached Brussels on the 2nd day of April, and a fortnight later reviewed his army. The French line drawn up in opposition to it suffered small but continual reverses until the close of the month.

On the 29th Clerfayt suffered a defeat which led to the fall, or rather the escape, of the small garrison of Menin. Clerfayt was beaten again at Courtray a fortnight later; but all these early engagements in the campaign were of no decisive moment. Tourcoing was to be the first heavy blow that should begin to settle matters, Fleurus was to clinch them.

No battle can be less satisfactorily described in a few lines than that of Tourcoing, so different did it appear to either combatant, so opposite are the plans of what was expected on either side, and of what happened, so confused are the various accounts of contemporaries. The accusations of treason which nearly always arise after a disaster, and especially a disaster overtaking an allied force, are particularly monstrous, and may be dismissed: in particular the childish legend which pretends that the Austrians desired an English defeat.

What the French say is that excellent forced marching and scientific concentration permitted them to attack the enemy before the junction of his various forces was effected. What the Allies say is (if they are speaking for their centre) that it was shamefully abandoned and unsupported by the two wings; if they are speaking for the wings, that the centre had no business to advance, when it saw that the two wings were not up in time to co-operate.

One story goes that the Archduke Charles was incapacitated by a fit; Lord Acton has lent his considerable authority to this amusing version. At any rate, what happened was this:—

The Allies lay along the river Scheldt on Friday, the 16th of May: Tournay was their centre, with the Duke of York in command of the chief force there; five or six miles north, down the river, was one extremity of their line at a place called Warcoing: it was a body of Hanoverians. The left, under the Archduke Charles, was Austrian and had reached a place a day's march south of Tournay called St. Amand. Over against the Allies lay a large French force also occupying a wide front of over fifteen miles, the centre of which was Tourcoing, then a village. Its left was in front of the fortress of Courtrai. Now, behind the French, up country northward in the opposite direction from the line of the Allies on the Scheldt was another force of the Allies under Clerfayt. The plan was that the Allied right should advance on to Mouscron and take it. The Allied centre should advance on to Tourcoing and Mouveaux and take them, while the left should march across the upper waters of the river Marque, forcing the bridges that crossed that marshy stream, and come up alongside the centre. In other words, there was to be an attack all along the French line from the south, and while it was proceeding, Clerfayt, from the north of the French, was to cross the Lys and attack also.

On the day of the 17th what happened was this: The left of the Allies, marching from St. Amand, came up half a day late; the right of the Allies took Mouscron, but were beaten out of it by the French. The centre of the Allies fulfilled their programme, reaching Tourcoing and its neighbourhood by noon and holding their positions. It is to the honour of English arms that this success was accomplished

Tourcoing.   May 16 to 18, 1794.

The breakdown of the attempt of the Allies to cut off the French near
Courtrai from Lille was due to their failure to synchronise. They should
have been in line from A to B at noon of the 17th with Clerfayt at C.

by a force a third of which was British and the most notable bayonet work in which was done by the Guards. Meanwhile, Clerfayt was late in moving and in crossing the river Lys, which lay between him and his objective.

When night fell, therefore, on the first day of the action, a glance at the map will show that instead of one solid line advancing against the French from A to B, and the northern force in touch with it at C, the Allied formation was an absurd projection in the middle, due to the success of the mixed and half-British force under the Duke of York: a success which had not been maintained on the two wings. A bulge of this sort in an attacking line is on the face of it disastrous. The enemy have only to be rapid in falling upon either flank of it and the bulge can be burst in. The French were rapid, and burst in the bulge was. By concentrating their forces against this one central part of the Allies they fought three to one.

That same capacity which at Wattignies had permitted them to scorn sleep and to be indefatigable in marching, put them on the road before three o'clock in the morning of Sunday, the 18th, and with the dawn they fell upon the central force of the Allies, attacking it from all three sides.

It is on this account that the battle is called the Battle of Tourcoing, for Tourcoing was the most advanced point to which the centre of the Allies had reached. The Germans, upon the Duke of York's right at Tourcoing, felt the first brunt of the attack. The Duke of York himself, with his mixed, half-British force, came in for the blow immediately afterwards, and while it was still early morning. The Germans at Tourcoing began to fall back. The Duke of York's force, to the left of them, was left isolated: its commander ought not to have hung on so long. But the defence was maintained with the utmost gallantry for the short time during which it was still possible. The retreat began about nine in the morning and was kept orderly for the first two miles, but after that point it was a rout. The drivers of the British cannon fled, and the guns, left without teams, blocked the precipitate flight of the cavalry. Their disorder communicated itself at once to the Guards, and to the line.

Even in this desperate strait some sort of order was restored, notably by the Guards Brigade, which were apparently the first to form, and a movement that could still be called a retreat was pursued towards the south. The Duke of York himself was chased from spinney to spinney and escaped by a stroke of luck, finding a bridge across the last brook held by a detachment of Hessians. In this way were the central columns, who between them numbered not a third of the total force of the Allies, destroyed.

Clerfayt had first advanced—but far too late to save the centre—and then retreated. The Archduke Charles, upon the left, was four hours late in marching to the help of the Duke of York; the right wing of the Allies was not even late: it spent the morning in an orderly artillery duel with the French force opposed to it. By five in the afternoon defeat was admitted and a general retreat of the Allies ordered.

I have said that many reasons are given to account for the disaster of Tourcoing, one of the very few in which a British force has been routed upon the Continent; but I confess that if I were asked for an explanation of my own, I would say that it was simply due to the gross

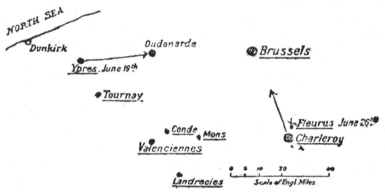

Showing effect of *Ypres*, *Charleroi* and *Fleurus* in wholly throwing back the Allies in June 1794.

Ypres captured on June 19 by the French, they march on Oudenarde and pass it on June 25 to 27. Meanwhile *Charleroi* has also surrendered to the French, and when, immediately afterwards, the Austrians try to relieve it, they are beaten at *Fleurus* and retire on Brussels.

Thus the English at *Tournai* and all the Allied Forces at *Condé*, *Valenciennes*, *Landrecies*, and *Mons* are imperilled and must surrender or retire.

lack of synchrony on the part of the Allies, and that this in its turn was taken advantage of by the power both of vigil and of marching which the French troops, still inferior in most military characteristics, had developed and maintained, and which (a more important matter) their commanders knew how to use.

This heavy blow, delivered on the 18th of May, in spite of a successful rally a week later, finally convinced the Emperor that the march on Paris was impossible. Eleven days later, on the 29th, it was announced in the camp of Tournay, upon which the Allied army had fallen back, that the Emperor had determined to return to Vienna. The Allied army was indeed still left upon that front, but the French continued to pour up against it. It was again their numbers that brought about the next and the final victory.

Far off, upon the east of that same line, the army which is famous in history and in song as that of the Sambre et Meuse was violently attempting to cross the Sambre and to turn the line of the Allies. Coburg reinforced his right opposite the French left, but numbers had begun to bewilder him. The enthusiasm of Saint-Just, the science of Carnot, decided victory at this eastern end of the line.

Six times the passage of the Sambre had failed. Reinforcements continued to reach the army, and the seventh attempt succeeded.

Charleroi, which is the main fortress blocking the passage of the Sambre at this place, could be, and was, invested when once the river was crossed by the French. It capitulated in a week. But the evacuation of Charleroi was but just accomplished when Coburg, seventy thousand strong, appeared in relief of the city.

Showing effect of Ypres, Charleroi and Fleurus in wholly throwing back the Allies in June 1794.

Ypres captured on June 19 by the French, they march on Oudenarde and pass it on June 25 to 27. Meanwhile Charleroi has also surrendered to the French, and when, immediately afterwards, the Austrians try to relieve it, they are beaten at Fleurus and retire on Brussels.

Thus the English at Tournai and all the Allied Forces at Condé, Valenciennes, Landrecies, and Mons are imperilled and must surrender or retire.

The plateau above the town where the great struggle was decided, is known as that of Fleurus, and it was upon the 26th of June that the armies were there engaged. Never before had forces so equal permitted the French any success. It had hitherto been the ceaseless requisitioning of men to supply their insufficient training and command, which had accomplished the salvation of the country. At Fleurus, though there was still some advantage on the French side, the numbers were more nearly equal.

The action was not determined for ten hours, and on the French centre and left was nearly lost, when the Reserves' and Marceau's obstinacy in front of Fleurus village itself at last decided it.

The consequences of the victory were final. As the French right advanced from Fleurus the French left advanced from Ypres, and the centre became untenable for the Allies. The four French fortresses which the enemy still garrisoned in that Belgian "belt" of which I have spoken, were invested and re-captured. By the 10th of July the French were in Brussels, the English were beaten back upon Holland, the Austrians retreating upon the Rhine, and the continuous success of the revolutionary armies was assured.

While these things were proceeding upon land, however, there had appeared a factor in the war which modern desire for comfort and, above all, for commercial security has greatly exaggerated, but which the student will do well to note in its due proportion. This factor was the military weakness of France at sea.

In mere numbers the struggle was entered upon with fleets in the ratio of about two to one, while to the fleet of Great Britain, already twice as large as its opponent, must be added the fleets of the Allies. But numbers did not then, nor will they in the future, really decide the issue of maritime war. It was the supremacy of English gunnery which turned the scale. This triumphant superiority was proved in the battle of the 1st of June, 1794.

The English fleet under Lord Howe attacked the French fleet which was waiting to escort a convoy of grain into Brest; the forces came in contact upon the 28th of May, and the action was a running one of three days.

Two examples must suffice to prove how determining was the superiority of the British fire. The *Queen Charlotte*, in the final action, found herself caught between the *Montagne* and the *Jacobin*. We have the figures of the losses during the duel of these two flagships. The *Queen Charlotte* lost forty-two men in the short and furious exchange, the *Montagne* alone three hundred. Again, consider the total figures. The number of the crews on both sides was nearly equal, but their losses were as eleven to five. It cannot be too often repeated that the initial advantage which the English fleet gained in the great war, which it maintained and increased as that war proceeded, and which it made absolute at Trafalgar, was an advantage mainly due to the guns.

The reader must not expect in a sketch which ends with the fall of Robespierre any treatise, however short, upon the effect of sea power in the revolutionary wars. It has of late years been grossly exaggerated, the reaction which will follow this exaggeration may as grossly belittle it. It prevented the invasion of England, it permitted the exasperation and wearing out of the French forces in the Peninsula. But it could not have determined the fate of Napoleon. That was determined by his

Russian miscalculation and by his subsequent and consequent defeat at Leipsic.

Upon the early success of the Revolution and the resulting establishment of European democracy, with which alone these pages deal, sea power was of no considerable effect.

CHAPTER VI

THE REVOLUTION AND THE CATHOLIC CHURCH

The last and the most important of the aspects which the French Revolution presents to a foreign, and in particular to an English reader, is the antagonism which arose between it and the Church.

As this is the most important so it is the most practical of the historical problems which the Revolution sets the student to solve; for the opposition of the Church's organisation in France has at once been the most profound which the Revolution has had to encounter, the most active in its methods, and the only one which has increased in strength as time proceeded. It is hardly too much to say that the Revolution would, in France at least, have achieved its object and created a homogeneous, centralised democracy, had not this great quarrel between the Republic and the Church arisen; and one may legitimately contrast the ready pliancy of men to political suggestion and the easy story of their institutions where men knew nothing of the Church, with the great storms that arise and the fundamental quarrels that are challenged wherever men are acquainted with the burning truths of Catholicism.

Finally, the struggle between the Catholic Church and the Revolution is not only the most important and the most practical, but also by an unhappy coincidence the most difficult of comprehension of all the matters presented to us by the great change. We have seen in this book that one department of revolutionary history, the second in importance, perhaps, to the religious department, was also difficult of comprehension—to wit, the military department. And we have seen (or at least I have postulated) that the difficulty of following the military fortunes of the Republic was due to the mass of detail, to the technical character of the information to be acquired and to the natural unfamiliarity of the general reader with the elements of military science. In other words, an accurate knowledge of great numbers of facts, the proper disposition of these facts in their order of military importance, and the correlation of a great number of disconnected actions and plans will alone permit us to grasp the function of the armies in the development and establishment of the modern State through the revolutionary wars.

Now in this second and greater problem, the problem of the function played by religion, it is an exactly opposite method which can alone be of service.

We must examine the field generally, and still more generally we must forget details that here only bewilder, and see in the largest possible outline what forces were really at issue, why their conflict occurred, upon what points that conflict was vital. Any more particular plan will land us, as it has landed so many thousands of controversialists, in mere invective on one side or the other, till we come to see nothing but a welter of treason on the part of priests, and of massacre upon the part of democrats.

Men would, did they try to unravel the skein by analysing the documents of the Vatican or of the French archives, come apparently upon nothing but a host of petty, base, and often personal calculations; or again, did they attempt to take a local sample of the struggle and to follow it in one department of thought, they would come upon nothing but a whirl of conflict with no sort of clue to the motives that lay behind.

The contrast between the military and the religious problem of the French Revolution is like the contrast between the geological composition and the topographical contours of a countryside. To understand the first we must bore and dig, we must take numerous samples of soil and subject them to analysis, we must make ourselves acquainted with detail in its utmost recesses. But for the second, the more general our standpoint, the wider our gaze, and the more comprehensive our judgment, the more accurately do we grasp the knowledge we have set out to seek.

We must, then, approach our business by asking at the outset the most general question of all: "*Was there a necessary and fundamental quarrel between the doctrines of the Revolution and those of the Catholic Church?*"

Those ill acquainted with either party, and therefore ill equipped for reply, commonly reply with assurance in the affirmative. The French (and still more the non-French) Republican who may happen, by the accident of his life, to have missed the Catholic Church, to have had no intimacy with any Catholic character, no reading of Catholic philosophy, and perhaps even no chance view of so much as an external Catholic ceremony, replies unhesitatingly that the Church is the necessary enemy of the Revolution. Again, the *émigré*, the wealthy woman, the recluse, any one of the many contemporary types to whom the democratic theory of the Revolution came as a complete novelty, and to-day the wealthy families in that tradition, reply as unhesitatingly that the Revolution is the necessary enemy of the Church. The reply seems quite sufficient to the Tory squire in England or Germany, who may happen to be a Catholic by birth or by conversion; and it seems equally obvious to (let us say) a democratic member of some Protestant Church in one of the new countries.

Historically and logically, theologically also, those who affirm a necessary antagonism between the Republic and the Church are in error. Those who are best fitted to approach the problem by their knowledge both of what the Revolution attempted and of what Catholic philosophy is, find it in proportion to their knowledge difficult or impossible to answer that fundamental question in the affirmative. They cannot call the Revolution a necessary enemy of the Church, nor the Church of Democracy.

What is more, minds at once of the most active and of the best instructed sort are the very minds which find it difficult to explain how any such quarrel can have arisen. French history itself is full of the names of those for whom not so much a reconciliation between the Revolution and the Church, as a statement that no real quarrel existed between them, was the motive of politics; and almost in proportion to a man's knowledge of his fellows in Catholic societies, almost in that proportion is the prime question I have asked answered by such a man in the negative. A man who knows both the Faith and the Republic will tell you that there is not and cannot be any necessary or fundamental reason why conflict should have arisen between a European Democracy and the Catholic Church.

When we examine those who concern themselves with the deepest and most abstract side of the quarrel, we find the same thing. It is impossible for the theologian, or even for the practical ecclesiastical teacher, to put his finger upon a political doctrine essential to the Revolution and to say, "This doctrine is opposed to Catholic dogma or to Catholic morals." Conversely, it is impossible for the Republican to put his finger upon a matter of ecclesiastical discipline or religious dogma and to say, "This Catholic point is at issue with my political theory of the State."

Thousands of active men upon either side would have been only too willing during the last hundred years to discover some such issue, and it has proved undiscoverable. In a word, only those Democrats who know little of the Catholic Church can say that of its nature it forbids democracy; and only those Catholics who have a confused or imperfect conception of democracy can say that of its nature it is antagonistic to the Catholic Church.

Much that is taught by the purely temporal theory of the one is indifferent to the transcendental and supernatural philosophy of the other. In some points, where there is contact (as in the conception of the dignity of man and of the equality of men) there is agreement. To sum up, the Republican cannot by his theory persecute the Church; the Church cannot by her theory excommunicate the Republican.

Why, then, it must next be asked, has there in practice arisen so furious and so enormous a conflict, a conflict whose activity and whose consequence are not narrowing but broadening to-day?

It may be replied to this second question, which is only less general than the first, in one of two manners.

One may say that the actions of men are divided not by theories but by spiritual atmospheres, as it were. According to this view men act under impulses not ideal but actual: impulses which affect great numbers and yet in their texture correspond to the complex but united impulses of an individual personality. Thus, though there be no conflict demonstrable between the theology of the Catholic Church and the political theory of the Revolution, yet there may be necessary and fundamental conflict between the *Persons* we call the Revolution and the Church, and between the vivifying principles by which either lives. That is one answer that can be, and is, given.

Or one may give a totally different answer and say, "There was no quarrel between the theology of the Catholic Church and the political theory of the Revolution; but the folly of this statesman, the ill drafting of that law, the misconception of such and such an institution, the coincidence of war breaking out at such and such a moment and affecting men in such and such a fashion—all these material accidents bred a misunderstanding between the two great forces, led into conflict the human officers and the human organisations which directed them; and conflict once established feeds upon, and grows from, its own substance."

Now, if that first form of reply be given to the question we have posed, though it is sufficient for the type of philosophy which uses it, though it is certainly explanatory of all human quarrels, and though it in particular satisfies a particular modern school of thought, it is evident that history, properly so called, cannot deal with it.

You may say that the Revolution was the expression of a spirit far more real than any theory, that this spirit is no more susceptible of analysis or definition than is the personality of a single human character, and that this reality was in conflict with another reality—to wit, the Catholic Church. You may even (as some minds by no means negligible have done) pass into the field of mysticism in the matter, and assert that really personal forces, wills superior and external to man, Demons and Angels, drove the Revolution against the Catholic Church, and created The Republic to be an anti-Catholic force capable of meeting and of defeating that Church, which (by its own definition of itself) is not a theory, but the expression of a Personality and a Will. To put it in old-fashioned terms, you may say that the Revolution was the work of antichrist;—but with that kind of reply, I repeat, history cannot deal.

If it be true that, in spite of an absence of contradictory intellectual theories, there is a fundamental spiritual contradiction between the Revolution and the Catholic Church, then time will test the business; we shall see in that case a perpetual extension of the quarrel until the Revolution becomes principally a force for the extinction of Catholicism, and the Catholic Church appears to the supporter of the Revolution not as his principal, but as his only enemy. Such a development has not arisen in a hundred years; a process of time far more lengthy will alone permit us to judge whether the supposed duello is a real matter or a phantasm.

The second type of answer, the answer which pretends to explain the antagonism by a definite series of events, does concern the historian.

Proceeding upon the lines of that second answer, he can bring his science to bear and use the instruments of his trade; and he can show (as I propose to show in what follows) how, although no quarrel can be found between the theory of the Revolution and that of the Church, an active quarrel did in fact spring up between the Revolution in action and the authorities of Catholicism; a quarrel which a hundred years has not appeased, but accentuated.

Behind the revolutionary quarrel lay the condition of the Church in the French State since the settlement of the quarrel of the Reformation.

With what that quarrel of the Reformation was, the reader is sufficiently familiar. For, roughly speaking, a hundred years, from the first years of the sixteenth century to the first years of the seventeenth (from the youth of Henry VIII to the boyhood of Charles I in England), a great attempt was made to change (as one party would have said to amend, as the other would have said to denaturalise) the *whole body* of Western Christendom. A *general* movement of attack upon the inherited form of the Church, and a general resistance to that attack, was at work throughout European civilisation; and either antagonist hoped for a universal success, the one of what he called "The Reformation of religion," the other of what he called "The Divine Institution and visible unity of the Catholic Church."

At the end of such a period it became apparent that no such general result had been, or could be, attained. All that part of the West which had rejected the authority of the See of Rome began to appear as a separate territorial region permanently divided from the rest; all that part of Europe which had retained the Authority of the See of Rome began to appear as another region of territory. The line of cleavage between the two was beginning to define itself as a geographical line, and nearly corresponded to the line which, centuries before, had divided the Roman and civilised world from the Barbarians.

The Province of Britain had an exceptional fate. Though Roman in origin and of the ancient civilisation in its foundation, it fell upon the non-Roman side of the new boundary; while Ireland, which the Roman Empire had never organised or instructed, remained, alone of the external parts of Europe, in communion with Rome. Italy, Spain, and in the main southern or Romanised Germany, refused ultimately to abandon their tradition of civilisation and of religion. But in Gaul it was otherwise—and the action of Gaul during the Reformation must be seized if its modern religious quarrels are to be apprehended. A very considerable proportion of the French landed and mercantile classes, that is of the wealthy men of the country, were in sympathy with the new religious doctrines and the new social organisation which had now taken root in England, Scotland, Holland, northern

Germany and Scandinavia, and which were destined in those countries to lead to the domination of wealth. These French squires and traders were called the Huguenots.

The succeeding hundred years, from 1615 to 1715, let us say, were a settlement, not without bloodshed, of the unsatisfied quarrel of the preceding century. All Englishmen know what happened in England; how the last vestiges of Catholicism were crushed out and all the social and political consequences of Protestantism established in the State.

There was, even in that same seventeenth century, a separate, but futile, attempt to destroy Catholicism in Ireland. In Germany a struggle of the utmost violence had only led to a similar regional result. The first third of that hundred years concluded in the Peace of Westphalia, and left the Protestant and Catholic territorial divisions much what we now know them.

In France, however, the peculiar phenomenon remained of a body powerful in numbers and (what was far more important) in wealth and social power, scattered throughout the territory of the kingdom, organised and, by this time, fixedly anti-Catholic, and therefore anti-national.

The nation had recovered its traditional line and had insisted upon the victory of a strong executive, and that executive Catholic. France, therefore, in this period of settlement, became an absolute monarchy whose chief possessed tremendous and immediate powers, and a monarchy which incorporated with itself all the great elements of the national tradition, *including the Church*.

It is the name of Louis XIV, of course, which symbolises this great time; his very long reign precisely corresponds to it. He was born coincidently with that universal struggle for a religious settlement in Europe, which I have described as characteristic of the time; he died precisely at its close; and under him it seemed as though the reconstructed power of Gaul and the defence of organised Catholicism were to be synonymous.

But there were two elements of disruption in that homogeneous body which Louis XIV apparently commanded. The very fact that the Church had thus become in France an unshakable national institution, chilled the vital source of Catholicism. Not only did the hierarchy stand in a perpetual suspicion of the Roman See, and toy with the conception of national independence, but they, and all the official organisation of French Catholicism, put the security of the national establishment and its intimate attachment to the general political structure of the State, far beyond the sanctity of Catholic dogma or the practice of Catholic morals.

That political structure—the French monarchy—seemed to be of granite and eternal. Had it indeed survived, the Church in Gaul would doubtless, in spite of its attachment to so mundane a thing as the crown, have still survived to enjoy one of those resurrections which have never failed it in the past, and would have returned, by some creative reaction, to its principle of life. But for the moment the consequence of this fixed political establishment was that scepticism, and all those other active forces of the mind which play upon religion in any Catholic State, had full opportunity. The Church was, so to speak, not concerned to defend itself but only its method of existence. It was as though a garrison, forgetting the main defences of a place, had concentrated all its efforts upon the security of one work which contained its supplies of food.

Wit, good verse, sincere enthusiasm, a lucid exposition of whatever in the human mind perpetually rebels against transcendental affirmations, were allowed every latitude and provoked no effective reply. But overt acts of disrespect to ecclesiastical authority were punished with rigour.

While in the wealthy, the bureaucratic, and the governing classes, to ridicule the Faith was an attitude taken for granted, seriously to attack the privileges or position of its ministers was ungentlemanly, and was not allowed. It did not shock the hierarchy that one of its Apostolic members should be a witty atheist; that another should go hunting upon Corpus Christi, nearly upset the Blessed Sacrament in his gallop, and forget what day it was when the accident occurred. The bishops found nothing remarkable in seeing a large proportion of their body to be loose livers, or in some of them openly presenting their friends to their mistresses as might be done by any great lay noble round them. That a diocese or any other spiritual charge should be divorced from its titular chief, seemed to them as natural as does to us the absence from his modern regiment of some titular foreign colonel. Unquestioned also by the bishops were the poverty, the neglect, and the uninstruction of the parish clergy; nay—and this is by far the principal feature—the abandonment of religion by all but a very few of the French millions, no more affected the ecclesiastical officials of the time than does the starvation of our poor affect, let us say, one of our professional politicians. It was a thing simply taken for granted.

The reader must seize that moribund condition of the religious life of France upon the eve of the Revolution, for it is at once imperfectly grasped by the general run of historians, and is also the only fact which thoroughly explains what followed. The swoon of the Faith in the eighteenth century is the negative foundation upon which the strange religious experience of the French was about to rise. France, in the generation before the Revolution, was passing through a phase in which the Catholic Faith was at a lower ebb than it had ever been since the preaching and establishment of it in Gaul.

This truth is veiled by more than one circumstance. Thus many official acts, notably marriages and the registration of births, took place under a Catholic form, and indeed Catholic forms had a monopoly of them. Again, the State wore Catholic clothes, as it were: the public occasions of pomp were full of religious ceremony. Few of the middle classes went to Mass in the great towns, hardly any of the artisans; but the Churches were "official." Great sums of money—including official money—were at the disposal of the Church; and the great ecclesiastics were men from whom solid favours could be got. Again, the historic truth is masked by the language and point of view of the great Catholic reaction which has taken place in our own time.

It is safe to say that where one adult of the educated classes concerned himself seriously with the Catholic Faith and Practice in France before the Revolution, there are five to-day. But in between lies the violent episode of the persecution, and the Catholic reaction in our time perpetually tends to contrast a supposed pre-revolutionary "Catholic" society with the revolutionary fury. "Look," say its champions, "at the dreadful way in which the Revolution treated the Church." And as they say this the converse truth appears obvious and they seem to imply, "Think how different it must have been before the Revolution persecuted the Church!" The very violence of the modern reaction towards Catholicism has exaggerated the revolutionary persecution, and in doing so has made men forget that apart from other evidence of the decline of religion, it is obvious that persecution could never have arisen without a strong and continuous historical backing. You could not have had a Diocletian in the thirteenth century with the spirit of the Crusaders just preceding him; you could not have had Henry VIII if the England of the fifteenth century just preceding him had been an England devoted to the monastic profession. And you could not have had the revolutionary fury against the Catholic Church in France if the preceding generation had been actively Catholic even in a considerable portion.

As a fact, of course it was not: and in the popular indifference to or hatred of the Church the principal factor was the strict brotherhood not so much of Church and State as of Church and executive Government.

But there was another factor. We were describing a little way back how in France there had arisen, during the movement of the Reformation, a wealthy, powerful and numerically large Huguenot body. In mere numbers it dwindled, but it maintained throughout the seventeenth century a very high position, both of privilege and (what was its characteristic) of money-power; and even to-day, though their birth-rate is, of course, lower than the average of the nation, the French Huguenots number close upon a million, and are far wealthier, upon the average, than their fellow citizens. It is their wealth which dominates the trade of certain districts, which exercises so great an effect upon the universities, the publishing trade, and the press; and in general lends them such weight in the affairs of the nation.

Now the Huguenot had in France a special and permanent quarrel with the monarchy, and therefore with the Catholic Church, which, precisely because it was not of the vivid and intense kind which is associated with popular and universal religions, was the more secretly ubiquitous. His quarrel was that, having been highly privileged for nearly a century, the member of "a State within a State," and for more than a generation free to hold assemblies separate from and often antagonistic to the national Government, these privileges had been suddenly removed from him by the Government of Louis XIV a century before the Revolution. The quarrel was more political than religious; it was a sort of "Home Rule" quarrel. For though the Huguenots were spread throughout France, they had possessed special cities and territories wherein their spirit and, to a certain extent, their private self-government, formed *enclaves* of particularism within the State.

They had held this position, as I have said, for close upon a hundred years, and it was not until a date contemporary with the violent settlement of the religious trouble in England by the expulsion of James II that a similar settlement, less violent, achieved (as it was thought) a similar religious unity in France. But that unity was not achieved. The

Huguenots, though no longer permitted to exist as a State within a State, remained, for the hundred years between the Revocation of the Edict of Nantes and the outbreak of the Revolution, a powerful and ever-watchful body. They stood upon the flank of the attack which intellectual scepticism was making upon the Catholic Church, they were prepared to take advantage of that scepticism's first political victory, and since the Revolution they have been the most powerful and, after the Freemasons, with whom they are largely identified, the most strongly organised, of the anti-clerical forces in the country.

The Jews, whose action since the Revolution has been so remarkable in this same business, were not, in the period immediately preceding it, of any considerable influence, and their element in the coalition may be neglected.

Such, then, was the position when the Revolution was preparing. Within memory of all men living, the Church had become more and more official, the masses of the great towns had wholly lost touch with it; the intelligence of the country was in the main drawn to the Deist or even to the purely sceptical propaganda, the powerful Huguenot body was ready prepared for an alliance with any foe of Catholicism, and in the eyes of the impoverished town populace—notably in Paris, which had long abandoned the practice of religion—the human organisation of the Church, the hierarchy, the priesthood, and the few but very wealthy religious orders which still lingered on in dwindling numbers, were but a portion of the privileged world which the populace hated and was prepared to destroy.

It is upon such a spirit and in such conditions of the national religious life that the Revolution begins to work. In the National Assembly you have the great body of the Commons which determines the whole, touched only here and there with men in any way acquainted with or devoted to Catholic practice, and those men for the most part individual and eccentric, that is, uncatholic, almost in proportion to the genuineness of their religious feeling. Among the nobility the practice of religion was a social habit with some—as a mental attitude the Faith was forgotten among all but a very few. Among the clergy a very wealthy hierarchy, no one of them prepared to defend the Church with philosophical argument, and almost unanimous in regarding itself as a part of the old political machine, was dominant; while the representatives of the lower clergy, strongly democratic in character, were at first more occupied with the establishment of democracy than with the impending attack upon the material and temporal organisation of the Church.

Now, that material and temporal organisation offered at the very beginning of the debates an opportunity for attack which no other department of the old *régime* could show.

The immediate peril of the State was financial. The pretext and even to some extent the motive for the calling of the States-General was the necessity for finding money. The old fiscal machinery had broken down, and as always happens when a fiscal machine breaks down, the hardship it involved, and the pressure upon individuals which it involved, appeared to be universal. *There was no immediate and easily available fund of wealth upon which the Executive could lay hands save the wealth of the clergy.*

The feudal dues of the nobles, if abandoned, must fall rather to the peasantry than to the State. Of the existing taxes few could be increased without peril, and none with any prospect of a large additional revenue. The charge for debt alone was one-half of the total receipts of the State, the deficit was, in proportion to the revenue, overwhelming. Face to face with that you had an institution not popular, one whose public functions were followed by but a small proportion of the population, one in which income was most unequally distributed, and one whose feudal property yielded in dues an amount equal to more than a quarter of the total revenue of the State. Add to this a system of tithes which produced nearly as much again, and it will be apparent under what a financial temptation the Assembly lay.

It may be argued, of course, that the right of the Church to this ecclesiastical property, whether in land or in tithes, was absolute, and that the confiscation of the one or of the other form of revenue was mere theft. But such was not the legal conception of the moment. The wealth of the Church was not even (and this is most remarkable) defended as absolute property by the generality of those who enjoyed it. The tone of the debates which suppressed the tithes, and later confiscated the Church lands, was a tone of discussion upon legal points, precedents, public utility, and so forth. There was not heard in it, in any effective degree, the assertion of mere moral right; though in that time the moral rights of property were among the first of political doctrines.

It was not, however, the confiscation of the Church lands and the suppression of the tithe which founded the quarrel between the Revolution and the clergy. No financial or economic change is ever more than a preparation for, or a permissive condition of, a moral change. It is never the cause of a moral change. Even the suppression of the religious houses in the beginning of 1790 must not be taken as the point of departure in the great quarrel. The religious orders in France were at that moment too decayed in zeal and in numbers, too wealthy and much too removed from the life of the nation, for this to be the case. The true historical point of departure from which we must date the beginning of this profound debate between the Revolution and Catholicism, is to be found in the morning of the 30th of May, 1790, when a parliamentary committee (the Ecclesiastical Committee) presented to the House its plan for the reform of the Constitution of the Church in Gaul.

The enormity of that act is now apparent to the whole world. The proposal, at the bidding of chance representatives not elected *ad hoc*, to change the dioceses and the sees of Catholic France, the decision of an ephemeral political body to limit to such and such ties (and very feeble they were) the bond between the Church of France and the Holy See, the suppression of the Cathedral Chapters, the seemingly farcical proposal that bishops should be elected, nay, priests also thus chosen, the submission of the hierarchy in the matter of residence and travel to a civil authority which openly declared itself indifferent in matters of religion,—all this bewilders the modern mind. How, we ask, could men so learned, so enthusiastic, so laborious and so closely in touch with all the realities of their time, make a blunder of that magnitude? Much more, how did such a blunder escape the damnation of universal mockery and immediate impotence? The answer is to be discovered in what has just been laid down with so much insistence: the temporary eclipse of religion in France before the Revolution broke out.

The men who framed the Constitution of the Clergy, the men who voted it, nay, even the men who argued against it, all had at the back of their minds three conceptions which they were attempting to reconcile: of those three conceptions one was wholly wrong, one was imperfect because superficial, the third alone was true. And these three conceptions were, first, that the Catholic Church was a moribund superstition, secondly, that it possessed in its organisation and tradition a power to be reckoned with, and thirdly, that the State, its organs, and their corporate inheritance of action, were so bound up with the Catholic Church that it was impossible to effect any general political settlement in which that body both external to France and internal, should be neglected.

Of these three conceptions, had the first been as true as the last, it would have saved the Constitution of the Clergy and the reputation for common-sense of those who framed it.

It was certainly true that Catholicism had for so many centuries been bound up in the framework of the State that the Parliament must therefore do something with the Church in the general settlement of the nation: it could not merely leave the Church on one side.

It was also superficially true that the Church was a power to be reckoned with politically, quite apart from the traditional union of Church and State—but only superficially true. What the revolutionary politicians feared was the intrigue of those who commanded the organisation of the Catholic Church, men whom they knew for the most part to be without religion, and the sincerity of all of whom they naturally doubted. A less superficial and a more solid judgment of the matter would have discovered that the real danger lay in the animosity or intrigue against the Civil Constitution, not of the corrupt hierarchy, but of the sincere though ill-instructed and dwindling minority which was still loyally attached to the doctrines and discipline of the Church. But even this superficial judgment would not have been fatal, had not the judgment of the National Assembly been actually erroneous upon the first point—the vitality of the Faith.

Had the Catholic Church been, as nearly all educated men then imagined, a moribund superstition, had the phase of decline through which it was passing been a phase comparable to that through which other religions have passed in their last moments, had it been supported by ancient families from mere tradition, clung to by remote peasants from mere ignorance and isolation, abandoned (as it was) in the towns simply because the towns had better opportunities of intellectual enlightenment and of acquiring elementary knowledge in history and the sciences; had, in a word, the imaginary picture which these men drew in their minds of the Catholic Church and its fortunes been an exact one, then the Civil Constitution of the Clergy would have been a statesmanlike act. It would have permitted the hold of the Catholic Church upon such districts as it still retained to vanish slowly and without shock. It proposed to keep alive at a reasonable salary the ministers of a ritual which would presumably have lost all

vitality before the last of its pensioners was dead; it would have prepared a bed, as it were, upon which the last of Catholicism in Gaul
could peacefully pass away. The action of the politicians in framing
the Constitution would have seemed more generous with every passing decade and their wisdom in avoiding offence to the few who still
remained faithful, would have been increasingly applauded.

On the other hand, and from the point of view of the statesman,
the Civil Constitution of the Clergy bound strictly to the State and
made responsible to it those ancient functions, not yet dead, of the
episcopacy and all its train. It was a wise and a just consideration
on the part of the Assembly that religions retain their machinery
long after they are dead, and if that machinery has ever been a State
machinery it must remain subject to the control of the State: and
subject not only up to the moment when the living force which once
animated it is fled, but much longer; up, indeed, to the moment when
the surviving institutions of the dead religion break down and perish.

So argued the National Assembly and its committee, and, I repeat,
the argument was just and statesmanlike, prudent and full of foresight,
save for one miscalculation. The Catholic Church was not dead, and
was not even dying. It was exhibiting many of the symptoms which in
other organisms and institutions correspond to the approach of death,
but the Catholic Church is an organism and an institution quite unlike
any other. It fructifies and expands immediately under the touch of
a lethal weapon; it has at its very roots the conception that material
prosperity is stifling to it, poverty and misfortune nutritious.

The men of the National Assembly would have acted more wisely
had they closely studied the story of Ireland (then but little known),
or had they even made themselves acquainted with the methods by
which the Catholic Church in Britain, after passing in the fifteenth
century through a phase somewhat similar to that under which it
was sinking in Gaul in the eighteenth, was stifled under Henry and
Elizabeth.

But the desire of the men of 1789 was not to kill the Church but
to let it die; they thought it dying. Their desire was only to make that
death decent and of no hurt to the nation, and to control the political
action of a hierarchy that had been wealthy and was bound up with
the old society that was crumbling upon every side.

The Civil Constitution of the Clergy failed: it lit the civil war, it dug
the pit which divided Catholicism from the Revolution at the moment

of the foreign invasion, it segregated the loyal priest in such a fashion that his order could not but appear to the populace as an order of traitors, and it led, in the furnace of 1793, to the great persecution from the memories of which the relations between the French democracy and the Church have not recovered.

It is important to trace the actual steps of the failure; for when we appreciate what the dates were, how short the time which was left for judgment or for revision, and how immediately disaster followed upon error, we can understand what followed and we can understand it in no other way.

If we find an enduring quarrel between two families whose cause of contention we cannot seize and whose mutual hostility we find unreasonable, to learn that it proceeded from a cataclysm too rapid and too violent for either to have exercised judgment upon it will enable us to excuse or at least to comprehend the endurance of their antagonism. Now, it was a cataclysm which fell upon the relations of the Church and State immediately after the error which the Parliament had committed; a cataclysm quite out of proportion to their intentions, as indeed are most sudden disasters quite out of proportion to the forces that bring them about.

It was, as we have seen, in the summer of 1790—upon the 12th of July—that the Civil Constitution of the Clergy was approved by the Assembly. But it was not until the 26th of August that the King consented to sign. Nor was there at the moment any attempt to give the law effect. The protests of the bishops, for instance, came out quite at leisure, in the month of October, and the active principle of the whole of the Civil Constitution—to wit, the presentation of the Civic Oath which the clergy were required to take, was not even debated until the end of the year.

This Civic Oath, which is sometimes used as a bugbear in the matter, was no more than an engagement under the sanction of an oath that the bishop or priest taking it would maintain the new *régime*— though that *régime* included the constitution of the clergy; the oath involved no direct breach with Catholic doctrine or practice. It was, indeed, a folly to impose it, and it was a folly based upon the ignorance of the politicians (and of many of the bishops of the day) as to the nature of the Catholic Church. But the oath was not, nor was it intended to be, a measure of persecution. Many of the parish clergy took it, and most of them probably took it in good faith: nor did it discredit the oath with the public that it was refused by all save four of the acting bishops, for the condition of the hierarchy in pre-revolutionary France was notorious. The action of the bishops appeared in the public eye to be purely political, and the ready acceptance of the oath by so many, though a minority, of the lower clergy argued strongly in its favour.

Nevertheless, no Catholic priest or bishop or layman could take that oath without landing himself in disloyalty to his religion; and that for the same reason which led St. Thomas of Canterbury to make his curious and fruitful stand against the reasonable and inevitable, as much as against the unreasonable, governmental provisions of his time. The Catholic Church is an institution of necessity autonomous. It cannot admit the right of any other power exterior to its own organisation to impose upon it a modification of its discipline, nor, above all, a new conception of its hieratic organisation.

The reader must carefully distinguish between the acceptation by the Church of a detail of economic reform, the consent to suppress a corporation at the request of the civil power, or even to forego certain traditional political rights, and the admission of the general principle of civil control. To that general principle the Assembly, in framing the Constitution of the Clergy, was quite evidently committed. To admit such a co-ordinate external and civil power, or rather to admit a *superior* external power, is in theory to deny the principle of Catholicism, and in practice to make of the Catholic Church what the other State religions of Christendom have become.

I have said that not until the end of the year 1790 was the debate opened upon the proposition to compel the clergy to take the oath.

It is a singular commentary upon the whole affair that compulsion should have been the subject for debate at all. It should have followed, one would have imagined, normally from the law. But so exceptional had been the action of the Assembly and, as they now were beginning to find, so perilous, that a special decree was necessary—and the King's signature to it—before this normal consequence of a measure which had been law for months, could be acted upon.

Here let the reader pause and consider with what that moment—the end of 1790—coincided.

The assignats, paper-money issued upon the security of the confiscated estates of the Church, had already depreciated 10 per cent. Those who had first accepted them were paying throughout France a penny in the livre, or as we may put it, a penny farthing on the shilling, for what must have seemed to most of them the obstinacy of one single corporation—and that an unpopular one—against the decrees of the National Assembly.

It was now the moment when a definite reaction against the Revolution was first taking shape, and when the populace was first beginning uneasily to have suspicion of it; it was the moment when the Court was beginning to negotiate for flight; it was the moment when (though the populace did not know it) Mirabeau was advising the King with all his might to seize upon the enforcement of the priests' oath as an opportunity for civil war.

The whole air of that winter was charged with doubt and mystery: in the minds of all who had enthusiastically followed the march of the Revolution, the short days of that rigorous cold of 1790–91 contained passages of despair, and a very brief period was to suffice for making the clerical oath not only the test of democracy against reaction, but the wedge that should split the nation in two.

With the very opening of the new year, on the 4th of January, the bishops and priests in the Assembly were summoned to take the oath to the King, the Nation, and the Law; but that law included the Civil Constitution of the Clergy, and they refused. Within three months Mirabeau was dead, the flight of the King determined on, the suspicion of Paris at white heat, the oath taken or refused throughout France, and the schismatic priests introduced into their parishes—it may be imagined with what a clamour and with how many village quarrels! In that same fortnight appeared the papal brief, long delayed, and known as the Brief "*Caritas*," denouncing the Civil Constitution of the Clergy. Six weeks later, at the end of May, the papal representative at the French Court was withdrawn, and in that act religious war declared.

Throughout this quarrel, which was now exactly of a year's duration, but the acute phase of which had lasted only six months, every act of either party to it necessarily tended to make the conflict more violent. Not only was there no opportunity for conciliation, but in the very nature of things the most moderate counsel had to range itself on one side or the other, and every public act which touched in any way upon the sore point, though it touched but indirectly, and with no desire on the part of the actors to rouse the passions of the moment, immediately appeared as a provocation upon one side or the other.

It was inevitable that it should be so, with a population which had abandoned the practice of religion, with the attachment of the clerical organisation to the organisation of the old *régime*, with the strict bond of discipline that united the priesthood of the Church in France into one whole, and above all with the necessity under which the Revolution was, at this stage, of finding a definite and tangible enemy.

This last point is of the very first importance. Public opinion was exasperated and inflamed, for the King was known to be an opponent of the democratic movement; yet he signed the bills and could not be overtly attacked. The Queen was known to be a violent opponent of it; but she did not actually govern. The Governments of Europe were known to be opponents; but no diplomatic note had yet appeared of which public opinion could make an object for attack.

The resistance, therefore, offered by the clergy to the Civil Constitution, had just that effect which a nucleus will have in the crystallisation of some solution. It polarised the energies of the Revolution, it provided a definite foil, a definite negative, a definite counterpoint, a definite butt. Here was a simple issue. Men wearing a special uniform, pursuing known functions, performing a known part in society—to wit, the priests—were now for the most part the enemies of the new democratic Constitution that was in preparation. They would not take the oath of loyalty to it: they were everywhere in secret rebellion against it and, where they were dispossessed of their cures, in open rebellion. The clergy, therefore, that is the non-juring clergy (and the conforming clergy were an experiment that soon became a fiction), were after April 1791, in the eyes of all the democrats of the time, the plainest and most tangible form of the opposition to democracy.

To the way in which I have presented the problem a great deal more might be added. The very fact that the democratic movement had come after a period of unfaith, and was non-Catholic in its springs, would have tended to produce that quarrel. So would the necessary attachment of the Catholic to authority and the easy confusion between the principle of authority and claims of a traditional monarchy. Again, the elements of vanity, of material greed, and of a false finality which are to be discovered in any purely democratic theory of the State, will between them always bring this theory into some conflict with religion. The centuries during which the throne and the altar had stood as twin symbols, especially in France, the very terminology of religious metaphor which had been forged during the centuries of monarchical institutions in Europe, helped to found the great quarrel. But, I repeat, the overt act without which the quarrel could never have become the terribly great thing it did, the master blunder which destroyed the unity of the revolutionary movement, was the Civil Constitution of the Clergy.

So much for the first year of the schism, May 1790 to May 1791. The second year is but an intensification of the process apparent in the first.

It opens with the King's flight in June 1791: that is, with the first open act of enmity taken against the authority of the National Parliament since, two years before, the National Parliament had declared itself supreme. Already the Court had been generally identified with the resistance of the clergy, and a particular example of this had appeared in the opinion that the King's attempted journey to St. Cloud in April had been prompted by a desire to have communion at the hands of a non-juring priest.* When, therefore, the King fled, though his flight had nothing whatsoever to do with the clerical quarrel, it was associated in men's minds with the clerical quarrel through his attempt to leave Paris in April and from a long association of the Court with the clerical resistance. The outburst of anti-monarchical feeling which followed the flight was at the same time an outburst of anti-clerical feeling; but the clergy were everywhere and could be attacked everywhere. The Declaration of Pillnitz, which the nation very rightly interpreted as the beginning of an armed European advance against the French democracy, was felt to be a threat not only in favour of the King but in favour also of the rebellious ecclesiastics.

And so forth. The uneasy approach of war throughout that autumn and winter of 1791–92, the peculiar transformation of the French temperament which war or its approach invariably produces—a sort of constructive exaltation and creative passion—began to turn a great part of its energy or fury against the very persons of the orthodox priests.

---

* This opinion has entered into so many Protestant and non-Catholic histories of the Revolution that it is worth criticising once again in this little book. The King was perfectly free to receive communion privately from the hands of orthodox priests, did so receive it, and had received communion well within the canonical times. There was little ecclesiastical reason for the attempted leaving of Paris for St. Cloud on Monday the 18th April, 1791, save the *custom* (not the religious duty) of communicating in public on Easter Sunday itself; it was a political move.

The new Parliament, the "Legislative" as it was called, had not been sitting two months when it passed, upon November 29, 1791, the decree that non-juring priests should be deprived of their stipend. And here again we must note the curious lack of adjustment between law and fact in all this clerical quarrel! For more than a year public money had been paid to men who, under the law, should not during the whole of that year have touched any salary! Yet, as in the case of the oath, special action was necessary, and moreover the Parliament added to this tardy and logical consequence of the law a declaration that those who had not so taken the oath within eight days of their decree should be rendered "suspect."

The word "suspect" is significant. The Parliament even now could not act, at least it could not act without the King; and this word "suspect," which carried no material consequences with it, was one that might cover a threat of things worse than regular and legal punishment. It was like the mark that some power not authorised or legal makes upon the door of those whom that power has singled out for massacre in some city.

Three weeks later Louis vetoed the decree refusing stipends to nonjurors, and the year 1791 ended with the whole matter in suspense but with exasperation increasing to madness.

The first three months of 1792 saw no change. The non-juring clergy were still tolerated by the Executive in their illegal position, and, what is more extraordinary, still received public money and were still for the most part in possession of their cures; the conception that the clergy were the prime, or at any rate the most obvious, enemies of the new *régime* now hardened into a fixed opinion which the attempted persecution of religion, as the one party called it, the obstinate and anti-national rebellion of factious priests, as the other party called it, was rapidly approaching real persecution and real rebellion.

With April 1792 came the war, and all the passions of the war.

The known hostility of the King to the Revolution was now become something far worse: his known sympathy with an enemy under arms. To force the King into the open was henceforward the main tactic of the revolutionary body.

Now for those whose object was forcing Louis XVI to open declarations of hostility against the nation, his religion was an obvious instrument. In no point could one come to closer grips with the King than on this question of the Church, where already, in December 1791, he had exercised his veto.

On May 27, 1792, therefore, Guadet and Vergniaud, the Girondins, moved that a priest who had refused to take the oath should be subjected to transportation upon the mere demand of any twenty taxpayers within that assembly of parishes known as a "Canton." It was almost exactly two years since the Civil Constitution of the Clergy had first been reported to the House by the Ecclesiastical Committee of the Constituent or National Assembly.

It must not be forgotten under what external conditions this violent act, the first true act of persecution, was demanded. It was already a month since, upon the 20th of April, the war had opened upon the Belgian frontier by a disgraceful panic and the murder of General Dillon; almost contemporaneous with that breakdown was the corresponding panic and flight of the French troops in their advance to Mons. All Europe was talking of the facile march upon Paris which could now be undertaken; and in general this decree against the priests was but part of the exasperated policy which was rising to meet the terror of the invasion.

It was followed, of course, by the decree dismissing the Royal Guard, and, rather more than a week later, by the demand for the formation of a camp of volunteers under the walls of Paris. But with this we are not here concerned. The King vetoed the decree against the non-juring priests, and in the wild two months that followed the orthodox clergy were, in the mind of the populace, and particularly the populace of Paris, identified with the cause of the re-establishment of the old *régime* and the success of the invading foreign armies.

With the crash of the 10th of August the persecution began: the true persecution, which was to the growing bitterness of the previous two years what a blow is to the opening words of a quarrel.

The decree of the 27th of May was put into force within eleven days of the fall of the Tuileries. True, it was not put into force in that crudity which the Parliament had demanded: the non-juring priests were given a fortnight to leave the kingdom, and if they failed to avail themselves of the delay were to be transported.

From this date to the end of the Terror, twenty-three months later, the story of the relations between the Revolution and the Church, though wild and terrible, is simple: it is a story of mere persecution culminating in extremes of cruelty and in the supposed uprooting of Christianity in France.

The orthodox clergy were everywhere regarded by this time as the typical enemies of the revolutionary movement; they themselves regarded the revolutionary movement, by this time, as being principally an attempt to destroy the Catholic Church.

Within seven months of the fall of the monarchy, from the 18th of March, 1793, the priests, whether non-juring or schismatic, might, on the denunciation of any six citizens, be subjected to transportation.

There followed immediately a general attack upon religion. The attempted closing of all churches was, of course, a failure, but it was firmly believed that such attachment as yet remained to the Catholic Church was due only to the ignorance of the provincial districts which displayed it, or to the self-seeking of those who fostered it. The attempt at mere "de-christianisation," as it was called, failed, but the months of terror and cruelty, the vast number of martyrdoms (for they were no less) and the incredible sufferings and indignities to which the priests who attempted to remain in the country were subjected, burnt itself, as it were, into the very fibre of the Catholic organisation in France, and remained, in spite of political theory one way or the other, and in spite of the national sympathies of the priesthood, the one great active memory inherited from that time.

Conversely, the picture of the priest, his habit and character, as the fatal and necessary opponent of the revolutionary theory, became so fixed in the mind of the Republican that two generations did nothing to eliminate it, and that even in our time the older men, in spite of pure theory, cannot rid themselves of an imagined connection between the Catholic Church and an international conspiracy against democracy. Nor does this non-rational but very real feeling lack support from the utterances of those who, in opposing the political theory of the French Revolution, consistently quote the Catholic Church as its necessary and holy antagonist.

The attempt to "de-christianise" France failed, as I have said, completely. Public worship was restored, and the Concordat of Napoleon was believed to have settled the relations between Church and State in a permanent fashion. We have lived to see it dissolved; but this generation will not see, nor perhaps the generation succeeding it, the issue of the struggle between two bodies of thought which are divided by no process of reason, but profoundly divorced by the action of vivid and tragic historical memories.

Made in United States
Orlando, FL
29 November 2023

39766326R00088